USDA

United States
Department of
Agriculture

Forest Service

Pacific Northwest
Research Station

General Technical Report
PNW-GTR-866

August 2012

California's Forest Products Industry and Timber Harvest, 2006

Todd A. Morgan, Jason P. Brandt, Kathleen E. Songster, Charles E. Keegan III, and Glenn A. Christensen

Authors

Todd A. Morgan is director of forest industry research, and **Kathleen E. Songster** and **Charles E. Keegan III** are research associates in the Bureau of Business and Economic Research, University of Montana, Gallagher Business Building, 32 Campus Dr. # 6840, Missoula, MT 59812-6840; **Jason P. Brandt** is a contract specialist, U.S. Department of Agriculture, Forest Service, National Interagency Fire Center, 3833 Development Ave., Boise, ID 83705-5354; and **Glenn A. Christensen** is a forester, U.S. Department of Agriculture, Forest Service, Pacific Northwest Research Station, Forestry Sciences Laboratory, 620 SW Main St., Suite 400, Portland, OR 97205.

Cover photographs: Top left: Self-loading truck preparing to take timber to the mill; top right: Even-aged harvest in northern California, 2004; bottom left: log deck and standing timber in northern California, 2004; bottom right photo: Bureau of Business and Economic Research Forester measuring felled trees at a logging site. Upper left photo by the Bureau of Business and Economic Research; all others by Todd Morgan.

Abstract

Morgan, Todd A.; Brandt, Jason P.; Songster, Kathleen E.; Keegan, Charles E., III; Christensen, Glenn A. 2012. California's forest products industry and timber harvest, 2006. Gen. Tech. Rep. PNW-GTR-866. Portland, OR: U.S. Department of Agriculture, Forest Service, Pacific Northwest Research Station. 48 p.

This report traces the flow of California's 2006 timber harvest through the primary wood products industry (i.e., firms that process timber into manufactured products such as lumber, as well as facilities such as pulp mills and particleboard plants, which use the wood fiber or mill residue directly from timber processors) and provides a description of the structure, condition, and economic impacts of California's forest products industry. Historical wood products industry changes are discussed, as well as trends in harvest, production, mill residue, and sales. Also examined are employment and worker earnings in the state's primary and secondary forest products industry.

Keywords: Bioenergy, employment, forest economics, lumber production, mill residue, mill capacity, wood products.

Highlights

- California's timber harvest was 1,733 million board feet (MMBF) Scribner during 2006. Nearly 60 percent (996 MMBF) of the timber harvest came from five counties. Humboldt County had the largest proportion at 20 percent (356 MMBF), followed by Shasta County with a timber harvest of 209 MMBF.

- A total of 77 primary forest products facilities operated in California during 2006. These included 33 sawmills, 25 bioenergy plants, 10 bark and mulch plants, 4 reconstituted board plants, 2 veneer plants, and 3 manufacturers of other primary wood products.

- Total sales value for California's primary forest products was about $1.5 billion in 2006, with lumber accounting for 64 percent of the total. The majority (70 percent) of all products was sold in California.

- Three sectors accounted for 94 percent of industry sales: sawmills, residue-utilizing plants, and bioenergy plants.

- California sawmills produced nearly 2.5 billion board feet of lumber in 2006, just under 7 percent of U.S. production of softwood lumber and nearly 4 percent of U.S. consumption.

- California's forest products industry's annual capacity to process sawtimber has decreased by nearly 70 percent, from 6 billion board feet Scribner in the late 1980s to 1.7 billion board feet in 2009.

- Approximately 78,100 workers, earning $4.4 billion annually, are employed in the primary and secondary wood and paper products industry in California.

- Total employment in California's wood and paper products industry has decreased since 1990, when employment was more than 105,000. Trends in labor income show similar declines from approximately $4.8 billion (in 2006 dollars) in labor income in 1990 to $4.4 billion in 2006. These long-term decreases have resulted almost entirely from losses in the primary industry.

Contents

Introduction

This report describes the structure, condition, and production of California's primary forest products industry for 2006, and discusses statewide timber harvest. Primary forest products manufacturers are firms that process timber into (manufactured) products such as lumber, as well as facilities such as pulp mills and particleboard plants that use the wood fiber or mill residue directly from timber processors. California's primary forest products include lumber, veneer, utility poles, and log home accents. Products made from chipping or grinding timber, as well as from mill residue (e.g., bark, sawdust, and planer shavings) generated in the production of primary products, also are included. These "reconstituted" primary products include pulp and paper, particleboard, medium-density fiberboard, and bioenergy. Derivative, or "secondary" products (i.e., goods made from primary products) such as window frames, doors, trusses, and furniture, are addressed only in the sales, employment, and earnings section of this report.

The principal goal of this study is to draw a detailed picture of the primary forest products industry in California and the timber it used during 2006. This includes tracking timber harvest from the forest through the manufacturing processes and into the marketplace. Detail is provided on type and quantity of primary manufacturers, harvest by product use as well as species, and geographic and ownership source of timber used. Mill production capacities and outputs, sales values, mill residues and their uses, and the general operating conditions facing the industry are presented. Historical trends in California's forest products industry are discussed as are the impacts of more recent downturns in housing and lumber markets.

The major source of data for this report is a statewide census of California's primary forest products industry and mills in nearby states that received timber harvested in California during calendar year 2006. The census, which is done approximately every 5 years, represents a cooperative effort between the University of Montana's Bureau of Business and Economic Research (BBER) and the U.S. Department of Agriculture (USDA) Forest Service, Pacific Northwest (PNW) Research Station, Forest Inventory and Analysis program.

Forest Industries Data Collection System

This report represents the second application of the Forest Industries Data Collection System (FIDACS) in the state of California. The first application was in 2000 (Morgan et al. 2004). The FIDACS consists of a census of all primary forest products manufacturers in a given state during a given year and the analysis and reporting of data collected from these firms. The firms surveyed were identified through participation in the previous study, telephone directories, directories of the forest products industry (Random Lengths 2006, RISI 2006), and with the assistance of the firms contacted. Through a written questionnaire or telephone interview, manufacturers provide the following information for each of their facilities:

- Facility type, location, contact information, and opening date
- Installed equipment and number of employees
- Number of operating days, shifts per day, and hours per shift
- Shift and annual production capacity in units of output
- Preferred and accepted log lengths and diameters
- Volume of raw material received by timber product, county, and ownership
- Species mix and proportion of standing dead timber received
- Raw material inventory at the beginning and end of the year
- Volume and destination of log transfers
- Finished product types, volumes, sales value, and market locations
- Finished product inventory at the beginning and end of the year
- Types, volumes, utilization, and sales of manufacturing residue

Manufacturers who participated in the 2006 California forest industry census processed all of the state's commercial timber harvest. Volume and other characteristics of timber processed by out-of-state facilities were determined through surveys of mills in adjacent states. Other data sources (Ehinger 2009, Random Lengths 2006, RISI 2006, U.S. Department of Commerce 2009, WWPA 2006) were used to estimate attributes for firms that did not complete the survey. Secondary information from federal, state, and private sources was used to verify estimates of the total timber harvest, lumber production, employment, and sales value of products.

Information collected through FIDACS is stored at the University of Montana's BBER in Missoula, Montana. Additional information is available by request. Individual firm-level data is confidential and cannot be released.

Overview of California's Forest Products Industry

California has been a major producer of wood products since attaining statehood in 1850. It emerged as the Nation's third leading softwood lumber-producing state in the 1940s, and since then has ranked second or third in the Nation, along with Oregon and Washington (Steer 1948, WWPA 1964–2009). Two major structural changes in California's forest products industry between 1945 and 1989 were the development and then near-disappearance of the plywood and veneer industries, and the development of other major wood products industries (i.e., pulp and paper, reconstituted board plants, decorative bark and mulch, and bioenergy) based on mill residue from sawmills and other major timber-processing facilities.

Operating Environment, 1945–2009

This section highlights changes in the operating environment that influenced California's forest products industry from 1945 to 2009. The relative recent past and historical trends are also discussed in this section.

California's forest products industry is continuously influenced by multiple factors, including U.S. and global economic forces, market conditions, timber inventories, public policy and regulations, and technological changes. Following World War II, timber harvest volumes expanded in response to the large increases in demand for lumber to supply the upsurge in U.S. home building. Abundant timber resources, industry diversification, and generally strong markets led to high harvest levels and growth in the value of mill output well into the 1970s. During the 1960s and 1970s, national forests became a key source of timber for California's industry. With reduced inventory available on private lands, the state's total harvest dropped about 15 percent from peaks in the late 1950s, and the proportion supplied by the national forests increased from just over 10 percent in the mid 1950s to over 40 percent by 1969. A severe recession and weak markets in the first half of the 1980s were followed by a substantial recovery in the last half of the 1980s. Mills in California benefited from these strong markets and an abundance of federal timber, boosting output and sales to unprecedented levels.

Restricted timber availability, particularly on federal lands, exerted a major influence on California's forest products industry after the 1980s. Harvests from federal timberland (mainly national forest land) declined 75 percent during the 1990s owing to numerous policy and legal constraints on timber harvesting. Private harvest was also lower in the 1990s, resulting largely from increasing state regulation of timber harvesting. Overall, California's timber harvest volume fell sharply throughout the 1990s. At the end of the decade, local and national markets for lumber and other wood products were strong, but in-state harvest was just over 2 billion board feet in 1999—less than half of the harvest levels of the late 1980s.

The years 2000 through 2002 saw weak U.S. and global economies, including a U.S. recession in 2001. This recession was made worse by the September 11 terrorist attacks. The expiration of the Canadian softwood lumber agreement and a strong U.S. dollar led to increased imports as lumber consumption in the U.S. remained stagnant. The increased lumber supply, which reduced domestic production, resulted in lower prices. In addition, very high and volatile electricity prices in 2000 and 2001 created problems for some California wood and paper products producers but opportunities for others. Mills buying electrical power from outside sources were faced with substantially higher operating costs. In contrast, a number

Harvests from federal timberland (mainly national forest land) declined 75 percent during the 1990s owing to numerous policy and legal constraints on timber harvesting.

of facilities using wood as fuel to produce electricity benefited by selling electricity to other users.

In the second half of 2003, wood product prices began to rise because of increased demand, both domestically and globally, as well as a weakening U.S. dollar. During 2004 and 2005, with U.S. housing starts exceeding 2 million annually, demand for wood products was strong and prices reached their highest level since the late 1990s. Strong global markets and hurricanes in the Southeastern United States brought additional demand for wood products. However, timber availability and an uncertain regulatory environment continued to affect California's forest products industry, and lumber output was actually lower in the strong market year of 2005 than in the recession year of 2001 (WWPA various years).

During 2006, a decline in U.S. housing construction led to sharp decreases in prices for most wood products. High fuel prices during the summer months contributed to higher logging and transportation costs. Many mills were forced to curtail production in 2006 because of market conditions. Owing to both ailing wood product markets and decreased timber availability, several large California mills closed between 2000 and 2006, and there was a net loss of production capacity in the state. New home starts decreased 40 percent from 2005 to 2007. Conditions worsened drastically in the last half of 2008, as falling home values and the high number of home foreclosures helped spur a severe global financial/credit crisis. This drove U.S. home starts in 2009 down to 554,000 units, the lowest level since the 1940s. The ongoing slump in housing has led to many temporary or indefinite curtailments and some permanent closures of California's wood product manufacturing facilities since 2006 (Random Lengths 2008 and 2009; WWPA 2008 and 2009).

Owing to both ailing wood product markets and decreased timber availability, several large California mills closed between 2000 and 2006, and there was a net loss of production capacity in the state.

California's Timber Harvest, Products, and Flow

This section discusses the ownership of California's timberlands, historical trends in California's timber harvest, and the wood products industry's use of timber, focusing on the year 2006. It presents ownership and geographic sources of timber, species composition, types of timber harvested and processed, utilization of wood fiber from the harvest, and movement of the resulting products both within California and between California and other states and countries.

Timber harvest data are available from several sources, including the California State Board of Equalization (annual) and the PNW Research Station of the USDA Forest Service (annual and periodic), and these sources were used for historical comparisons. However, detailed harvest volumes presented in this report for 2006 are the result of a full census of California and out-of-state mills receiving timber harvested in California during 2006. Differences may exist between the numbers published here and those published by other sources. These differences are often the result of differing reporting units and conversion factors, rounding error, scaling discrepancies among timber sellers (agencies and private owners) and between sellers and buyers, and other reporting variations.

Timber harvested from California timberland came from three broad land ownership categories: industrial timberland, nonindustrial private forest (NIPF) land, and public lands. California's timber harvest consisted largely of true firs (*Abies* spp.), Douglas-fir (*Pseudotsuga menziesii* (Mirb.) Franco), ponderosa pine (*Pinus ponderosa* Dougl. ex Laws.), redwood (*Sequoia sempervirens* (D. Don) Endl.), sugar pine (*Pinus lambertiana* Dougl.), western hemlock (*Tsuga heterophylla* (Raf.) Sarg.), incense-cedar (*Calocedrus decurrens* (Torr.) Florin.), and Jeffrey pine (*Pinus jeffreyi* Balf.). Most timber used by California's industry was harvested from within the state, with additional volume coming from Oregon. Some smaller volumes came from Washington and Canada.

California's Timberlands

California has approximately 99.6 million acres of land area, of which 33.2 million acres are forested (Christensen et al. 2008, Miles and Hansen 2008). Of the total forest land in California, private landowners hold 13.0 million acres (39 percent), national forest lands account for 15.8 million acres (48 percent), and other public lands account for the remaining 13 percent or 4.2 million acres. Approximately 19.5 of the 33.2 million forested acres in California are classified as timberland. Timberland is forest land that is producing or capable of producing more than 20 cubic feet of wood per acre per year at culmination of mean annual increment and excludes reserved lands (Society of American Foresters 1998). National forests contain 9.8 million acres (51 percent) of timberland, private landowners hold approximately 8.9 million acres (45 percent), and the remaining 4 percent (less than 1 million acres) is held by other public landowners (fig. 1).

In 2006, California's timberlands contained approximately 304 billion board feet Scribner of sawtimber (Christensen et al. 2008). Sawtimber is timber of "sufficient size and quality to be suitable for conversion into lumber" (Random Lengths 1993). Sawtimber volume is calculated from growing-stock trees that are at least 11 inches diameter at breast height (d.b.h.) for hardwoods, and 9 inches d.b.h. for softwoods. Measured in Scribner board feet, live sawtimber on timberland is 94 percent conifers, with hardwoods at 6 percent. By species, Douglas-fir accounts for 33 percent of the Scribner board foot sawtimber volume on timberland. Other species contributing the majority of volume on timberland are true fir (22 percent), ponderosa and Jeffrey pines (18 percent), redwood (8 percent), and sugar pine (5 percent).

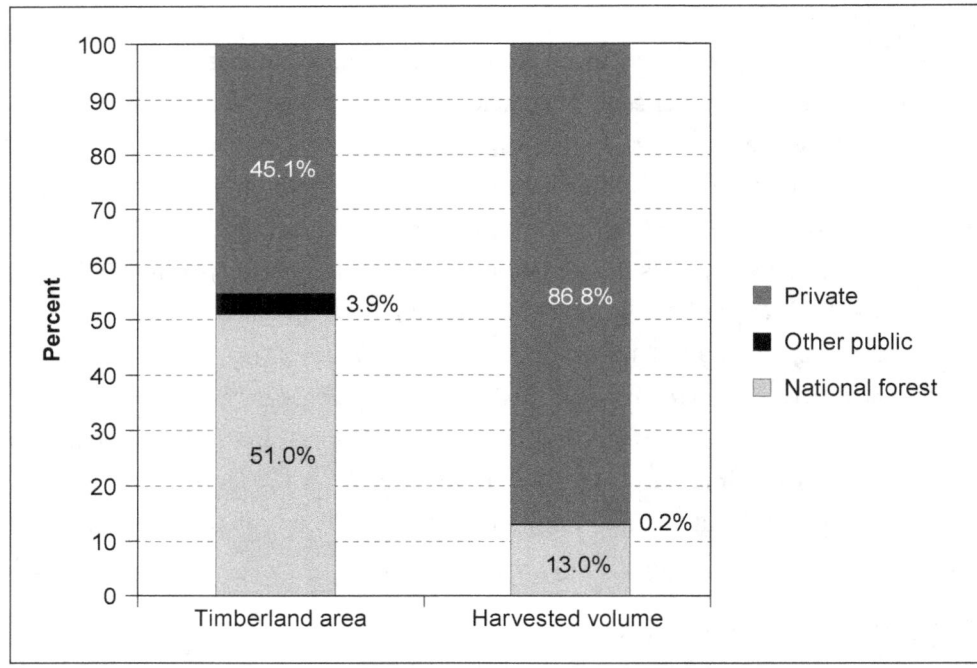

Figure 1—Characteristics of California's timberland by ownership class, 2006.

Harvest by Ownership

The timber volume harvested in California during 2006 was 1.7 billion board feet Scribner (table 1), a decline of about 23 percent from the 2000 harvest of 2.2 billion board feet (Morgan et al. 2004). The timber harvest during 2006 was less than 62 percent of the average volume of the previous 20 years, and less than 45 percent of the average over the last 50 years. Industrial landowners provided the majority (54 percent) of the timber harvest, with NIPF (32 percent) and national forests (13 percent) providing nearly all of the remaining volume.

Private lands have provided the majority of California's timber since the 1940s (figs. 2 and 3). However, during the 1960s, 1970s, and 1980s, as private harvest

Table 1—California's timber harvest by ownership class, 2006

Ownership	Harvest[a]	Percentage of total
	Million board feet	*Percent*
Industrial	942.7	54.40
Nonindustrial private	555.8	32.07
National forest	224.7	12.96
Tribal	5.6	0.32
State	3.5	0.20
Bureau of Land Management	0.3	0.02
Other public	0.4	0.02
Total	1,733.1	100.00

[a] Volume in Scribner Decimal C Log Rule, eastside variant.

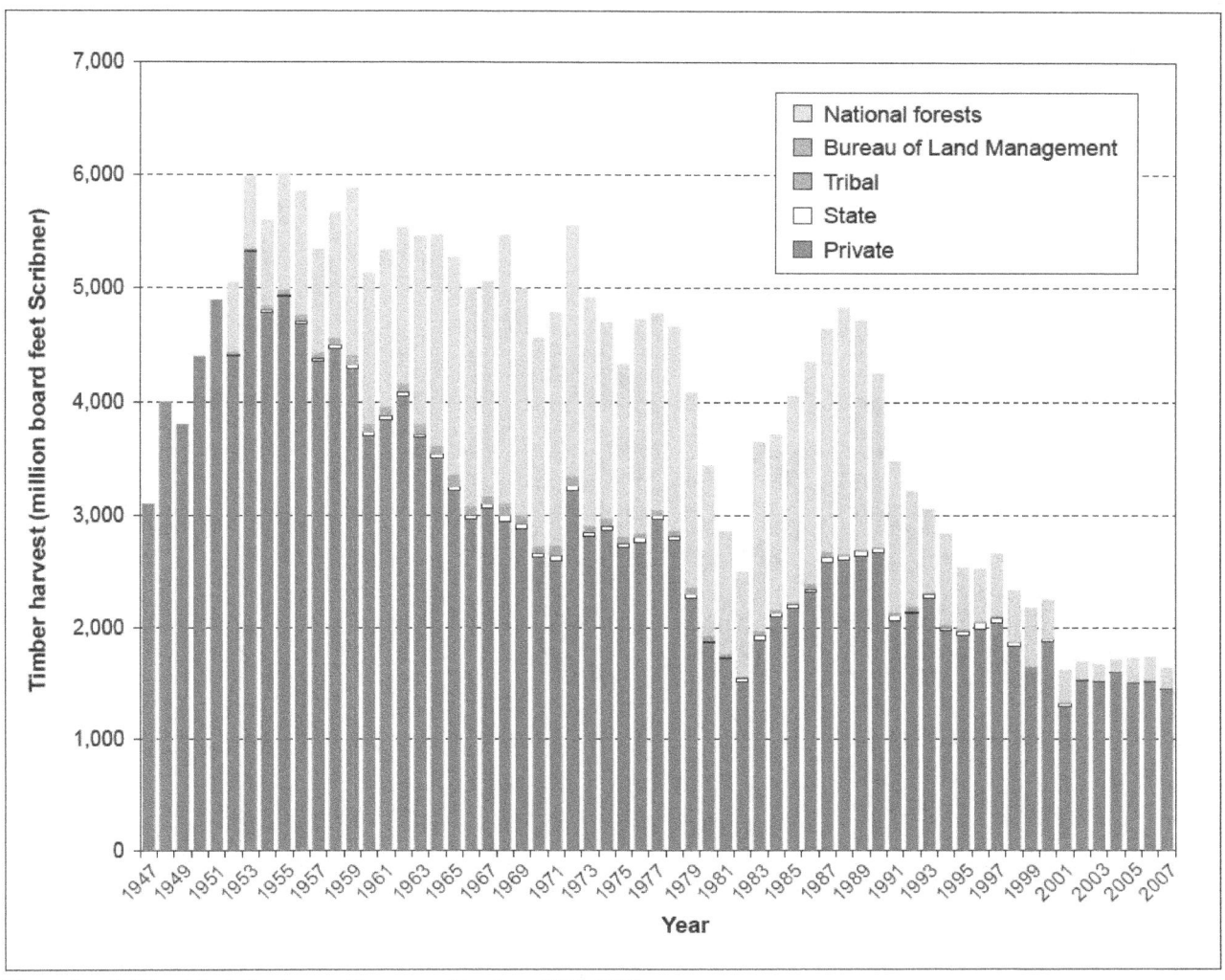

Figure 2—California's timber harvest by ownership class, 1947–2007.

volumes declined, national forests became an increasingly important source of timber for California's industry and the Nation's growing demand for housing and wood products. National forest timber offerings were fairly constant during these decades (averaging about 1.8 billion board feet Scribner), but the proportion of total harvest supplied by national forests increased from just over 10 percent in the mid 1950s to about 45 percent in the late 1980s. Total timber harvest volume in California declined about 15 percent during this period.

Since the late 1980s, both private and national forest harvests have declined, with reductions in national forest harvest accounting for the majority (1.8 billion board feet) of the 3-billion-board-foot total decline. Harvests from federal timberland (mainly national forests) declined by 1.5 billion board feet during the 1990s and an additional 300 million board feet (MMBF) Scribner by 2007. The major causes of

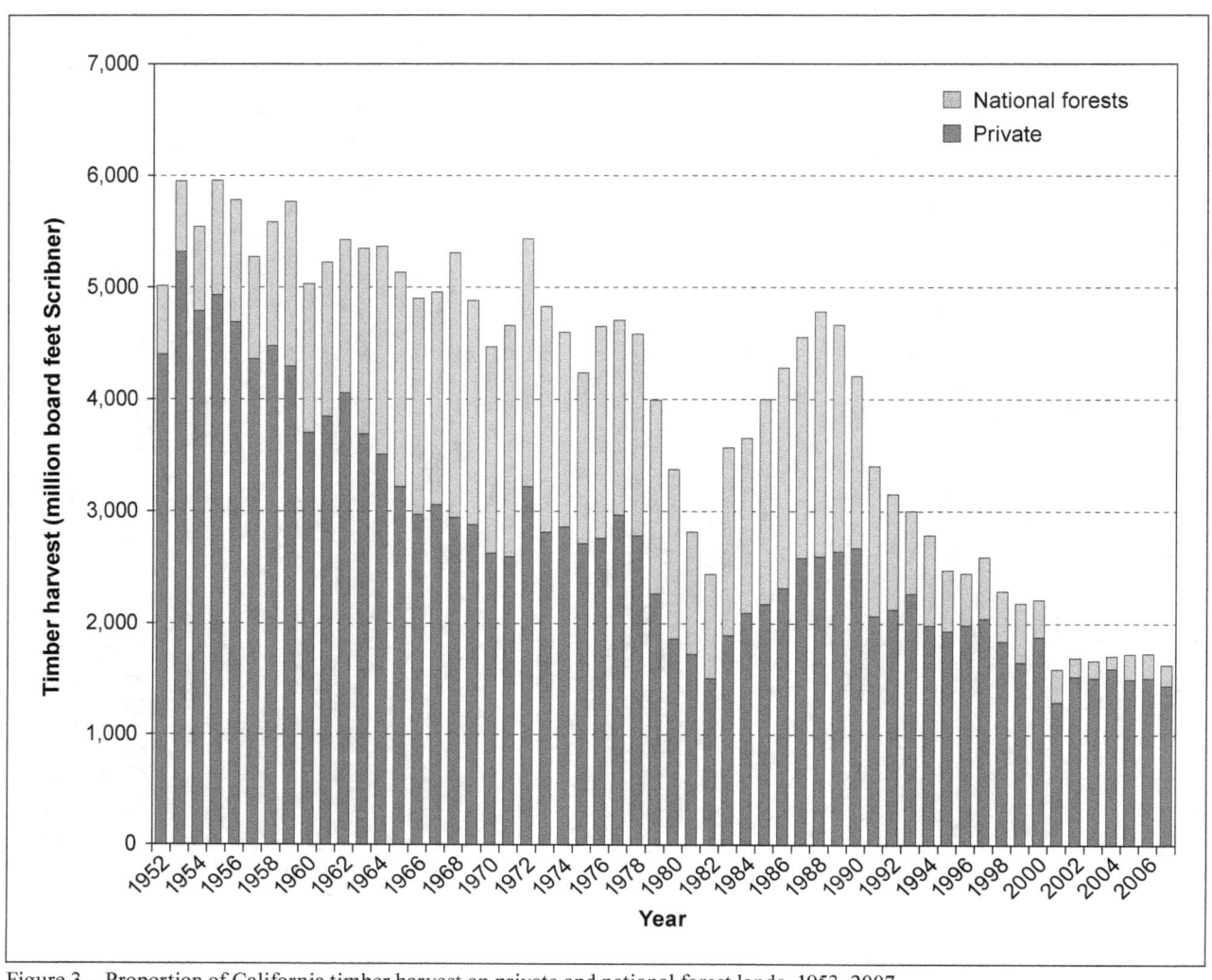

Figure 3—Proportion of California timber harvest on private and national forest lands, 1953–2007.

declines in national forest timber offerings since the 1980s have been social, political, and legal constraints on harvesting. The proportion of national forest timber
in the share of California's total harvest also dropped sharply from over 45 percent
in the late 1980s to 15 percent in 2000, 13 percent in 2006, and about 11 percent in
2007 (fig. 3). Relating these harvest percentages to California's timberland ownership, national forests supply less than 15 percent of the harvest volume from 51
percent of the state's timberland, thus more than 85 percent of the harvest volume is
coming from the remaining 49 percent of California timberland (fig. 1).

Private harvest in California dropped from more than 2.5 billion board feet in
the late 1980s to less than 1.5 billion board feet during the mid to late 2000s, resulting largely from increased regulation, set asides for old-growth forest protection, and
various other social and political pressures, not because of wood products markets.

Timber harvest volumes from national forest timber lands in California, like private lands, declined throughout the 1990s and first half of the 2000s even as demand for housing and wood products consumption in California and the United States increased substantially. Likewise, the 35 percent decline in new housing starts between 2005 and 2007 had surprisingly little impact on timber harvest levels in California, with harvest volume only falling about 6 percent from the peak home-building years of 2005 through 2007.

Harvest by Geographic Source

Six multicounty resource areas are used to describe major wood-producing regions in California (fig. 4): North Coast, Northern Interior, Sacramento, San Joaquin, Central Coast, and Southern California. In 2006, 91 percent (1.5 billion board feet) of California's total timber harvest (1.7 billion board feet) came from the North Coast, Northern Interior, and Sacramento regions. Historically, these regions have provided more than 85 percent of California's timber harvest (Barrette et al. 1970;

Figure 4—California's forest resource areas.

California State Board of Equalization 1992–2007; Hiserote and Howard 1978; Howard 1974, 1984; Howard and Ward 1988, 1991; Morgan et al. 2004; Ward 1995, 1997). Virtually all of the remaining timber harvest in 2006 came from the San Joaquin region.

Five counties in northern California accounted for over 57 percent of California's total timber harvest in 2006 (table 2). The timber harvest in each county exceeded 120 MMBF Scribner during that year. These proportions are virtually unchanged since 2000, when these same counties contributed about 55 percent of the total harvest (Morgan et al. 2004).

In 2006, Humboldt County had the largest timber harvest at 346 MMBF. Shasta County's harvest was about 209 MMBF, Siskiyou County accounted for 196 MMBF, and Mendocino and Plumas Counties each had about 122 MMBF harvested during the year. Humboldt County has typically had the largest harvest, around 20 percent of the annual total (table 3). Other counties that have also generally been top producers include Mendocino, Plumas, Shasta, Siskiyou, and Trinity (Barrette et al. 1970; Hiserote and Howard 1978; Howard 1974, 1984; Howard and Ward 1988, 1991; Morgan et al. 2004; Ward 1995, 1997).

Harvest by Species

During 2006, true firs, Douglas-fir, ponderosa pine, redwood, and sugar pine were the most commonly harvested tree species, accounting for 90 percent of California's total harvest volume (table 4). These species have dominated California's harvest, consistently accounting for 85 percent or more of the total (table 5). The major change from 2000 was an increase in true firs from 19 to 28 percent of the harvest accompanied by modest declines in the contributions of Douglas-fir and redwood. These recent changes are in line with long-term trends, which show proportionate decreases in Douglas-fir and redwood and increases in true firs with the pines maintaining a relatively consistent share.

Harvest by Product Type

Products directly manufactured from timber are referred to as primary products. These include lumber, plywood, veneer, posts and poles, pilings and timbers, and cedar shakes and shingles. Products made from chipping or grinding timber, as well as from the residues (e.g., bark, sawdust, and planer shavings) generated in the production of primary products, also are included. These reconstituted primary products include pulp and paper, particleboard, medium-density fiberboard, hardboard, and bioenergy. In this report, timber product classification is based on the primary product manufactured directly from timber in roundwood form.

Table 2—California's timber harvest by county, 2000 and 2006

Resource area	2000 volume[a]	2000 percentage of total[a]	2006 volume	2006 percentage of total
	Million board feet[b]	*Percent*	*Million board feet[b]*	*Percent*
Central Coast:				
Napa	—	—	0.3	*c*
San Benito	—	—	0.1	*c*
San Mateo	5.6	0.3	4.4	0.3
Santa Clara	4.2	0.2	4.4	0.3
Santa Cruz	19.6	0.9	9.7	0.6
Total Central Coast	29.4	1.3	18.8	1.1
North Coast:				
Del Norte	50.4	2.2	17.6	1.0
Humboldt	435.3	19.3	345.7	19.9
Mendocino	193.5	8.6	123.1	7.1
Sonoma	28.1	1.2	9.9	0.6
Total North Coast	707.2	31.4	496.3	28.6
Northern Interior:				
Lassen	69.3	3.1	77.9	4.5
Modoc	49.9	2.2	26.3	1.5
Shasta	194.3	8.6	209.0	12.1
Siskiyou	209.7	9.3	196.0	11.3
Trinity	99.6	4.4	98.0	5.7
Total Northern Interior:	622.6	27.7	607.2	35.0
Sacramento:				
Butte	86.4	3.8	89.2	5.1
El Dorado	106.7	4.7	99.1	5.7
Glenn	24.7	1.1	4.9	0.3
Lake	9.6	0.4	1.6	0.1
Nevada	59.6	2.6	39.4	2.3
Placer	40.4	1.8	47.4	2.7
Plumas	193.8	8.6	122.4	7.1
Sierra	33.1	1.5	16.3	0.9
Tehama	105.3	4.7	45.7	2.6
Yolo	2.6	0.1	—	—
Yuba	36.9	1.6	7.2	0.4
Total Sacramento	699.0	31.1	473.3	27.3
San Joaquin:				
Alpine	—	—	*c*	*c*
Amador	22.8	1.0	28.7	1.7
Calaveras	67.0	3.0	34.9	2.0
Fresno	19.8	0.9	5.9	0.3
Kern	3.6	0.2	—	—
Madera	4.8	0.2	0.1	*c*
Mariposa	3.6	0.2	3.7	0.2
Merced	0.3	*c*	—	—
Tulare	8.9	0.4	7.7	0.4
Tuolumne	60.7	2.7	47.2	2.7
Total San Joaquin	191.4	8.5	128.1	7.4
Southern California:				
San Bernardino	—	—	9.55	0.55
Total southern California	0	0	9.6	0.6
State total	2,249.7	100.0	1,733.1	100.0

[a] Source: Morgan et al. 2004.
[b] Volume in Scribner Decimal C Log Rule, eastside variant.
[c] Volume is less than .05 MMBF or percentage of total harvest is less than .05%.

Table 3—Percentage of total harvest for California's leading timber harvest counties, 1968–2006

County	Volume[a]	Percentage of total
	Million board feet	*Percent*
1968:		
Humboldt	1,186.8	21.7
Mendocino	533.4	9.7
Siskiyou	502.6	9.2
Trinity	431.6	7.9
Shasta	381.1	7.0
Total county	3,035.5	55.5
California total	5,473.0	
1972:		
Humboldt	1,079.0	19.9
Mendocino	523.1	9.6
Siskiyou	518.7	9.5
Del Norte	354.5	6.5
Trinity	349.9	6.4
Total county	2,825.2	52.0
California total	5,435.2	
1976:		
Humboldt	1,073.3	22.7
Mendocino	489.2	10.3
Shasta	359.3	7.6
Siskiyou	337.1	7.1
Del Norte	236.4	5.0
Total county	2,495.3	52.7
California total	4,731.0	
1982:		
Humboldt	456.2	18.3
Mendocino	448.1	17.9
Plumas	164.7	6.6
Trinity	161.2	6.5
Tehama	148.3	5.9
Total county	1,378.5	55.2
California total	2,497.0	
1985:		
Humboldt	608.1	15.0
Mendocino	435.1	10.7
Shasta	204.1	5.0
Plumas	202.2	5.0
Siskiyou	201.8	5.0
Total county	1,651.3	40.7
California total	4,056.0	

Table 3—Percentage of total harvest for California's leading timber harvest counties, 1968–2006 (continued)

County	Volume[a]	Percentage of total
	Million board feet	*Percent*
1988:		
Humboldt	769.0	15.9
Mendocino	499.1	10.3
Siskiyou	295.6	6.1
Trinity	272.1	5.6
Plumas	271.5	5.6
Total county	2,107.3	43.5
California total	4,840.0	
1992:		
Humboldt	502.2	15.6
Mendocino	271.6	8.5
El Dorado	195.1	6.1
Lassen	158.8	4.9
Shasta	142.9	4.4
Total county	1,270.6	39.5
California total	3,214.0	
1994:		
Humboldt	559.6	19.7
Plumas	163.5	5.8
Shasta	147.5	5.2
Lassen	123.3	4.3
Trinity	117.2	4.1
Total county	1,111.1	39.1
California total	2,839.0	
2000:		
Humboldt	435.3	19.3
Siskiyou	209.7	9.3
Shasta	194.3	8.6
Plumas	193.8	8.6
Mendocino	193.5	8.6
Total county	1,226.6	54.5
California total	2,249.7	
2006:		
Humboldt	345.7	20.0
Shasta	209.0	12.1
Siskiyou	196.0	11.3
Mendocino	123.1	7.1
Plumas	122.4	7.1
Total county	996.2	57.5
California total	1,733.1	

[a] Volume in Scribner Decimal C Log Rule, eastside variant

Source: Barrette et al. 1970; Hiserote and Howard 1978; Howard 1974, 1984; Howard and Ward 1988, 1991; Morgan et al. 2004; Ward 1995, 1997.

Table 4—California's timber harvest by species, 2006

Species	Volume[a]	Percentage of total
	Million board feet	*Percent*
True firs	491	28.3
Douglas-fir	419	24.2
Ponderosa pine	301	17.4
Redwood	247	14.3
Sugar pine	99	5.7
Incense-cedar	83	4.8
Other softwoods	68	3.9
Western hemlock	25	1.4
Hardwoods	1	0.04
All species	1,733	100.00

[a] Volume in Scribner Decimal C Log Rule, eastside variant.

Timber harvested in California falls into five general timber product categories: sawlogs (timber used to produce lumber and other sawn products), veneer logs (timber sliced or peeled to make veneer for plywood or laminated veneer lumber), bioenergy (timber burned industrially to generate electricity or steam), pulpwood (timber used to manufacture pulp, paper, and reconstituted boards), and other products. Timber harvested for export is addressed under the "Timber Flow" section of this report.

Sawlogs accounted for 88 percent (1,528 MMBF) of the harvest in 2006. Historically, sawlogs have accounted for more than 85 percent of the total annual harvest (table 6). Veneer logs accounted for 10 percent of the total harvest through the 1970s. Since the 1980s, however, veneer logs have accounted for only 4 to 8 percent of California's annual timber harvest with the 2006 veneer log harvest at 8 percent.

Table 5—Percentage of California's timber harvest by species, 1968–2006[a]

Species	1968	1972	1976	1982	1985	1988	1992	1994	2000	2006
					Percent					
True firs	22.4	21.8	19.9	21.1	22.0	23.0	22.9	25.6	19.0	28.3
Douglas-fir	32.2	26.9	27.4	22.9	24.1	26.5	23.2	26.7	27.6	24.2
Ponderosa and sugar pine	23.7	25.3	25.4	27.0	26.3	26.9	23.4	22.0	23.8	23.1
Redwood	18.2	18.7	19.5	24.3	22.6	18.2	24.9	21.9	16.7	14.3
Other softwoods[b]	3.3	3.0	3.6	0.5	1.4	1.3	1.3	1.3	7.7	5.4
Incense-cedar	[c]	4.1	4.1	3.9	3.0	3.7	4.3	2.4	4.7	4.8
Hardwoods	0.2	0.2	0.2	0.4	0.5	0.5	[d]	[d]	0.5	[d]
Total	100	100	100	100	100	100	100	100	100	100

[a] Harvest for years prior to 2000 does not include timber delivered to out-of-state mills.
[b] Other softwoods include western hemlock, lodgepole pine, spruces, and other coniferous species.
[c] Included in "Other softwoods."
[d] Less than 0.05 percent.
Source: Barrette et al. 1970; Hiserote and Howard 1978; Howard 1974, 1984; Howard and Ward 1988, 1991; Morgan et al. 2004; Ward 1995, 1997.

Table 6—Percentage of California's timber harvest by product type, 1968–2006[a]

Product type	1968	1972	1976	1982	1985	1988	1992	1994	2000	2006
	- *Percent* -									
Sawlogs	86	86	86	91.2	92	92.5	99.3	92.9	89.8	88.1
Veneer logs	10	12	11.5	6.1	5	4.7	*b*	5.2	7.4	8.0
Pulpwood	1	1.5	0.1	1.1	0.8	1.1	*c*	*c*	*c*	*c*
Other[d]	3	0.5	2.4	1.6	2.2	1.7	0.7	1.9	0.4	>0.3
Bioenergy	*e*	*e*	*e*	*e*	*e*	*e*	*e*	*e*	2.4	3.6
Total	100	100	100	100	100	100	100	100	100	100

[a] Harvest for years prior to 2000 does not include timber delivered to out-of-state mills.
[b] Included in "sawlogs."
[c] Included in "other."
[d] Includes shakes and shingles, posts and poles, utility poles, houselogs, and log export; does not include bioenergy.
[e] Not reported prior to 2000.
Source: Barrette et al. 1970; Hiserote and Howard 1978; Howard 1974, 1984; Howard and Ward 1988, 1991; Morgan et al. 2004; Ward 1995, 1997.

Generally, timber harvested for products other than sawlogs and veneer logs has represented a small portion of California's annual total harvest. Bioenergy has been an expanding use of California's timber in recent years, with 3.6 percent (62.2 MMBF) of the harvest volume delivered to bioenergy producers in 2006. Bioenergy accounted for 2.4 percent (54.6 MMBF) of timber harvest in 2000. Prior to 2000, mill surveys did not identify timber harvested specifically to produce energy. Pulpwood accounted for less than 2 percent of the annual harvest volume because of the pulp and board sector's heavy reliance on mill residues. Pulpwood harvest has declined further in recent years with the closure of one of the two pulp mills operating in the state during 2000. Logs harvested for other products, like shakes and shingles, posts and poles, and house log components, have accounted for less than 3 percent of the annual harvest.

Bioenergy has been an expanding use of California's timber in recent years.

Product Type by Ownership Source

As discussed earlier, most of the volume harvested in 2006 came from private timberlands (table 7). Sawlogs were the most often harvested product from all ownership groups. In 2006, private lands provided 87 percent (1,455 MMBF) of California's saw and veneer log harvest; in 2000, private lands contributed 84 percent (1,836 MMBF) (Morgan et al. 2004). For 2006, Industrial lands were the largest private supplier of saw, veneer, and other logs, at 898 MMBF; and national forests were the primary supplier of timber from public lands, accounting for 212 MMBF. Wood for bioenergy came primarily from industrial land as well, accounting for about 73 percent (45.1 MMBF) of the total volume harvested for bioenergy. National forests accounted for about 21 percent of the bioenergy harvest (13.1 MMBF).

Table 7—California's timber harvest by ownership source and product type, 2006

Ownership source	Sawlogs	Veneer and other[a]	Bioenergy	All products
	- - - - - - - - - - - - - *Million board feet[b]* - - - - - - - - - - - - - - - -			
Private timberlands:	1,327.3	127.8	49.1	1,504.2
Industrial	801.2	96.5	45.1	942.7
Nonindustrial	520.5	31.3	4.1	555.8
Tribal	5.6	—	—	5.6
Public timberlands:	200.5	15.3	13.1	228.9
National forests	200.2	11.5	13.1	224.7
Other public	0.4	3.9	—	4.3
Total	1,527.8	143.1	62.2	1,733.1

[a] Other product types include houselogs and utility poles.
[b] Volume in Scribner Decimal C Log Rule, eastside variant.

Minor differences exist between timber volume harvested in California (table 7) and the volume received by mills in California because of timber flowing into and out of state (table 8). This movement is described further in the section on timber flow. In 2006, California's sawmill, veneer, and other plants received 1,730.8 MMBF of logs. Of that volume, 83 percent came from private timberlands, about 12 percent came from national forests, and 4 percent came from other ownerships. Bioenergy facilities in California received about 62 MMBF of timber, in addition to mill residue. Approximately 72 percent of that timber came from industrial lands, about 21 percent from national forests, and the rest from nonindustrial private. The residue-utilizing sector (reconstituted board and decorative bark facilities) did not receive any timber and used mill residues exclusively for their raw material.

Table 8—Timber products received by California's forest industry sectors by ownership source, 2006[a]

Ownership source	Sawlogs	Veneer and other[b]	Bioenergy	All products
	- - - - - - - - - - - - - - - *Million board feet[c]* - - - - - - - - - - - - - - -.-			
Private timberlands:	1,328.0	121.1	49.1	1,498.2
Industrial	837.2	91.6	45.1	974.0
Nonindustrial	485.8	29.5	4.1	519.3
Tribal	5.0	—	—	5.0
Public timberlands:	199.6	22.4	13.1	235.1
National forests	199.3	12.2	13.1	224.6
Other public	0.3	10.2	—	10.5
Canada:	59.7	—	—	59.7
Total	1,587.3	143.5	62.2	1,793.0

[a] Reported volume is net exports.
[b] Other product types include houselogs and utility poles.
[c] Volumes in Scribner Decimal C Log Rule, eastside variant.

Product Type by Species

In 2006, true firs and Douglas-fir were the species most harvested for saw and veneer logs, and other softwoods were the most harvested species for bioenergy (table 9). In 2000, other softwoods accounted for more than 85 percent (53 MMBF) of timber used for bioenergy but just under 4 percent for all products. Approximately 7 percent of timber harvested for bioenergy was ponderosa pine and about 4 percent was true firs. Douglas-fir, incense-cedar, and hardwoods made up the rest of the species used for bioenergy in 2006. During 2000, Douglas-fir was the most used for saw and veneer logs, and true firs accounted for 48 percent of timber used for bioenergy at 26 MMBF (Morgan et al. 2004). Similar to 2000, hardwoods comprised very little (less than 0.05 percent) of the 2006 harvest and were primarily used for sawlogs and bioenergy.

End Uses of California's 2006 Timber Harvest

This section traces California's timber harvest through the various product manufacturing sectors. Because both timber products and mill residue from manufacturing facilities are presented, volumes are expressed in cubic feet rather than board feet Scribner. Residue volumes were reported in bone-dry units (BDU = 2,400 pounds of oven-dry wood) and converted to cubic feet by using a conversion of 96 cubic feet per BDU (Hartman et al. 1981). Timber harvest volumes of bole wood were generally reported in board feet Scribner Decimal C eastside variant. Different conversion factors were applied to combine these disparate volume measures into cubic-foot volume. The following conversion factors were developed using log size

Table 9—California's timber harvest by species and product type, 2006

Species	Sawlogs	Veneer and other[a]	Bioenergy	All products	Percentage of total
		-- Million board feet[b] --			
True firs	404.7	83.8	2.5	491.0	28.3
Douglas-fir	386.2	31.6	0.9	418.7	24.2
Ponderosa pine	280.3	16.4	4.3	301.1	17.4
Redwood	247.1	—	—	247.1	14.3
Sugar pine	97.8	1.3	—	99.2	5.7
Incense-cedar	81.4	0.1	1.1	82.6	4.8
Other softwoods	6.0	9.1	53.1	68.2	3.9
Western hemlock	23.8	0.8	—	24.6	1.4
Hardwoods	0.4	—	0.3	0.7	0.04
All species	1,527.8	143.1	62.2	1,733.1	100

[a] Other product types include houselogs and utility poles.
[b] Volumes in Scribner Decimal C Log Rule, eastside variant.
— = Values less than 0 1 thousand board feet.

specifications as well as product and residue recovery information developed from the 2006 FIDACS mill survey in California:

- 5.35 board feet per cubic foot for sawlogs.
- 1.0 board feet per cubic foot for bioenergy logs.
- 5.0 board feet per cubic foot for veneer and other logs.

California's 2006 timber harvest was approximately 375 million cubic feet (MMCF) of bole wood. Approximately 286 MMCF (76 percent) went to sawmills and was processed into lumber and other sawn products, and about 29 MMCF (8 percent) went to veneer and plywood facilities (fig. 5). Also included in the veneer category are small volumes (less than 2 MMCF) that went to other primary processors, including utility pole plants and log home accent facilities. Bioenergy plants received 60 MMCF of timber and 21 MMCF of mill residue from other plants processing California timber. The pulp and paper industry did not use any timber harvested in roundwood form but received substantial volumes of mill residue generated from sawmills and other primary processors in California.

Figure 5 shows that of the 286 MMCF of timber received by sawmills, 136 MMCF (48 percent) became finished lumber and about 7 MMCF was lost to lumber shrinkage, with 143 MMCF remaining as mill residue. Most of the mill residue generated by sawmills processing California timber went to pulp and board manufacturers (56 MMCF) and bioenergy facilities (19 MMCF). The majority of the remaining mill residue was used internally for fuel (53 MMCF), with 15 MMCF going to other uses such as animal bedding. A very small amount, less than 0.05 MMCF of residue from processing California timber into lumber, was unused in 2006, and is not included in figure 5. This compares to 5 MMCF of unused residue in 2000 (Morgan et al. 2004).

During 2006, 29 MMCF of bole wood was delivered to veneer and plywood facilities in California. About 55 percent (16 MMCF) became veneer and other finished products, 31 percent (9 MMCF) became residue that was sold to pulp and board manufacturers, and the remaining 14 percent (4 MMCF) became other products such as peeler cores or was used internally for energy.

Since 2000, there was a decrease in the total amount of wood fiber from California used by the bioenergy sector and the pulp and board industry. This overall decrease in wood fiber resulted from the decreased harvest of sawlogs and veneer logs and subsequent decrease of mill residue. However, the volume of timber harvested specifically for bioenergy rose, increasing from 55 MMCF in 2000 to 61 MMCF in 2006. In 2000, the harvest of roundwood delivered directly to pulp and board mills was 3 MMCF; in 2006, no California timber was harvested and sent directly to the pulp and board industry.

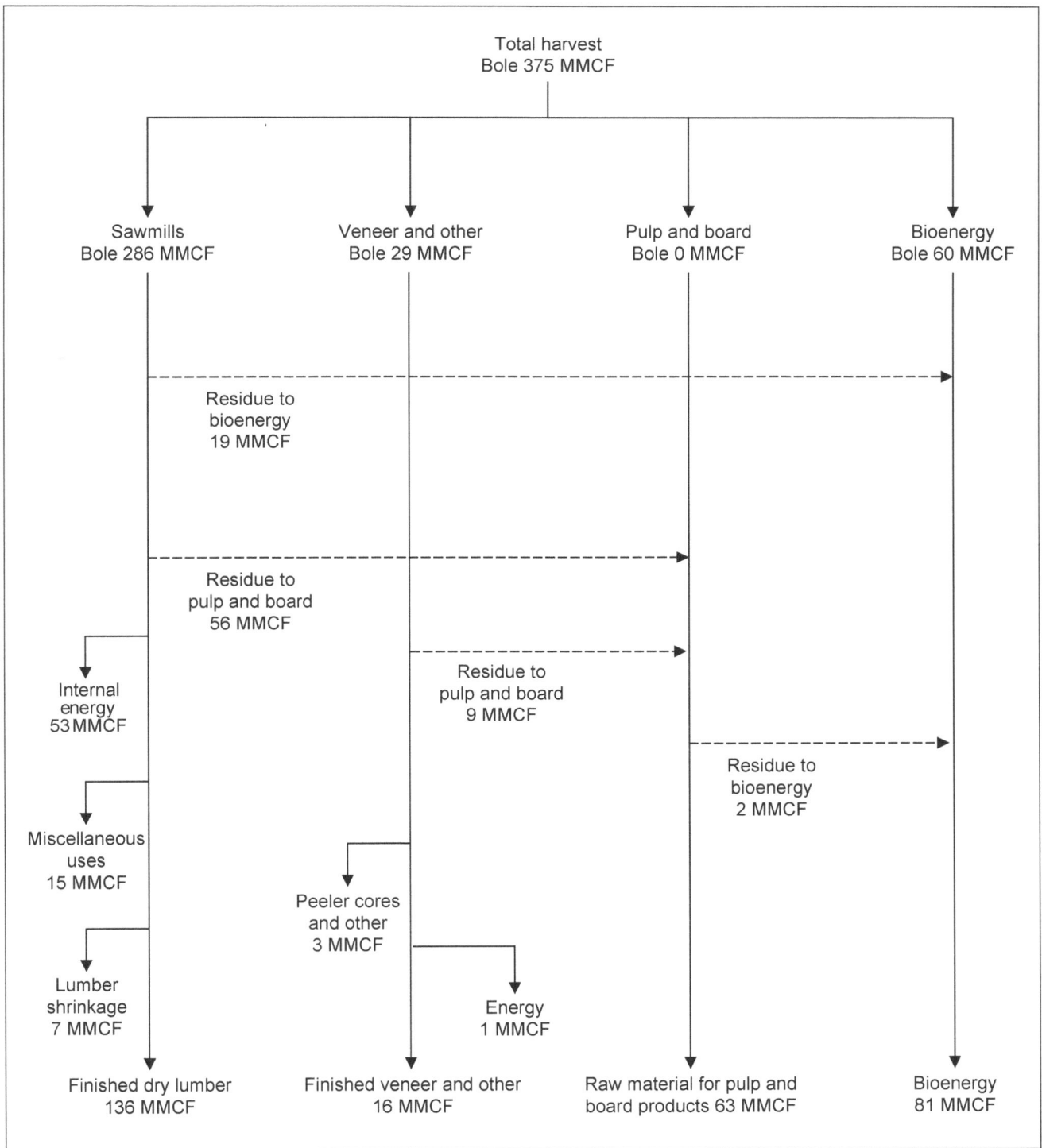

Figure 5—Utilization of California's timber harvest, 2006. MMCF = million cubic feet.

In total, 375 MMCF of wood fiber (bole wood) was harvested from California timberlands in 2006. The timber was utilized as follows:

- 136 MMCF became finished lumber
- 135 MMCF were used to generate biomass energy, usually in the form of steam or electricity
- 63 MMCF were used as raw material to produce pulp and paper or reconstituted board products such as particleboard or medium-density fiberboard
- 16 MMCF became veneer or plywood
- 18 MMCF went to other uses such as animal bedding
- 7 MMCF were lost in shrinkage from green to dry lumber

Figure 6 demonstrates this final disposition of wood fiber harvested in California during 2006.

Timber Flow

This section briefly details the movement of timber among California's wood-producing regions, resource areas, and individual counties, as well as between California and other states. Because this study tracks timber flowing into and out of the state, there are slight differences in the amount of timber harvested versus received by facilities in the state (tables 7 and 8).

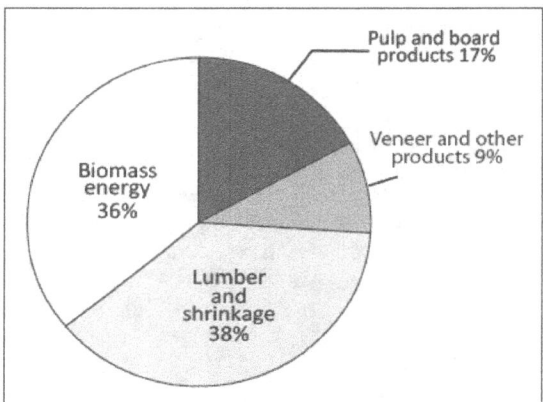

Figure 6—Final disposition of wood harvested in California by industry sector.

California timber-processing facilities received nearly 1.8 billion board feet of timber in 2006. Slightly less than 127 MMBF or approximately 7 percent of timber processed in California came from out of state, whereas slightly less than 67 MMBF or nearly 4 percent of California's timber harvest was processed in Oregon, making California a net importer of about 60 MMBF of timber in 2006 (table 10).

Table 10—California's timber imports and exports, 2006

Timber products	Imports	Exports[a]	Net imports
	---------- Million board feet ---------		
Saw and veneer logs	126.5	(66.5)	60.0
Bioenergy and other[b] logs	< 0.05	0	< 0.05
Total	126.5	(66.6)	59.9

[a] Volume in Scribner Decimal C Log Rule, eastside variant.
[b] Other logs include timber harvested for houselogs and utility poles.

Over 99 percent of the timber that flowed into California and all the timber that flowed out was saw and veneer logs. These volumes do not include approximately 16 MMBF of logs exported internationally from California's customs districts (WWPA 2007).

International and Interstate Timber Flows

The use of foreign timber by California timber processors rose between 2000 and 2006. In 2006 California mills received 59.7 MMBF of timber from Canada, accounting for 3.3 percent of the timber processed in California (table 11). In 2000, California facilities imported 20.6 MMBF of timber, again entirely from Canada. Past reports (Barrette et al. 1970; Hiserote and Howard 1978; Howard 1974; Howard and Ward 1988, 1991; Ward 1995) do not indicate any timber entering California from international sources, although timber entering California from other states increased substantially from the late 1960s through the 1990s.

The volumes of timber harvested in California, exported from California, and processed in California have been declining since the 1960s, while the volume of imported timber began rapidly increasing in the early 1990s (fig. 7). From the late 1960s through 1985, imports of timber from other states more than doubled, in-state timber harvest decreased 26 percent, log exports declined by 70 percent, and the volume of timber processed in-state declined by 40 percent. Between 1988 and 2006, timber harvest dropped by another 61 percent. Imports of out-of-state and Canadian timber have increased substantially and account for more than 6 percent of the annual volume processed in California during recent years.

Table 11—Ownership source of timber volume received by California mills, 2006

Ownership source	Volume	Percentage of total
	Million board feet[a]	*Percent*
Private timberlands:	1,498.20	83.6
Industrial	974	54.3
Nonindustrial	519.3	29.0
Tribal	5	0.3
Public timberlands:	235.1	13.1
National forests	224.6	12.5
Other	10.5	0.6
Canada:	59.7	3.3
Total	1,793.0	100.0

[a] Volume in Scribner Decimal C Log Rule, eastside variant.

These trends reflect a situation that many western mills have wrestled with— difficulty finding sufficient locally available timber to meet demand for finished wood products. During the strong upward trend in housing during the 1990s and first half of the 2000s, timber processors in California struggled because of changes in the availability of timber from private as well as public lands. To compensate, in-state mills have increasingly been procuring timber from out-of-state, particularly from Oregon, Washington, and Canadian sources to ensure that their raw material needs are met.

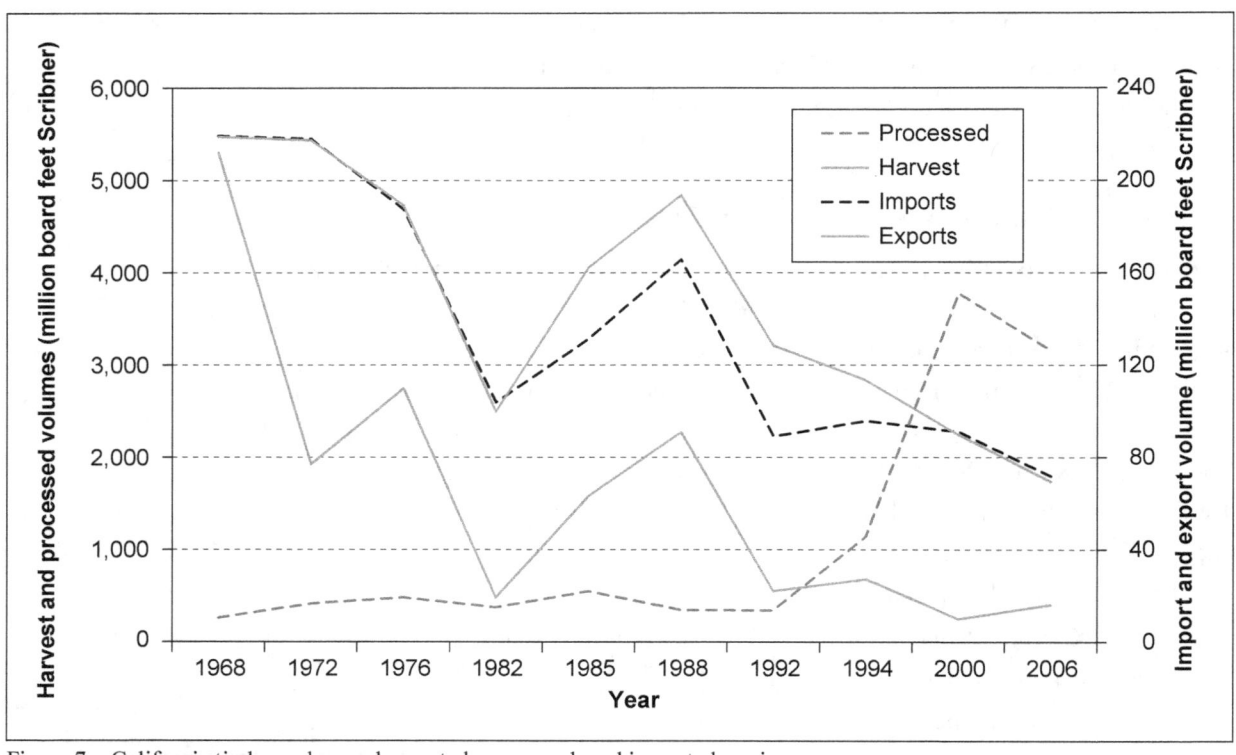

Figure 7—California timber volumes: harvested, processed, and imported, various years.

In recent years, international export of timber from California ports has made up a very small percentage of the annual harvest (fig. 8). From 1999 to 2007, the average annual export was 9.8 MMBF, less than 0.5 percent of the annual timber harvest during the period (WWPA 1999–2007). This reporting body does not indicate how much, if any, of the wood was actually harvested in California. The peak for international log exports originating in California was in 1968, at 4 percent (202.4 MMBF) of the total harvest.

Intrastate Timber Flow

This section briefly examines the flow of California timber to mills within the state. Several counties have too few timber-processing facilities to avoid disclosure of firm-level data, so individual county statistics are not reported for all counties (table 12).

Reflecting tighter timber supplies and the development of larger mills, not only has the volume of timber imported into California increased, but timber harvested and processed within California is travelling farther today than in the past. During 2000 and 2006, less than one-half of harvested timber was processed in its county of harvest, and approximately 82 percent was processed in the resource area of harvest. By comparison, in 1968, 74 percent of the volume harvested and used by

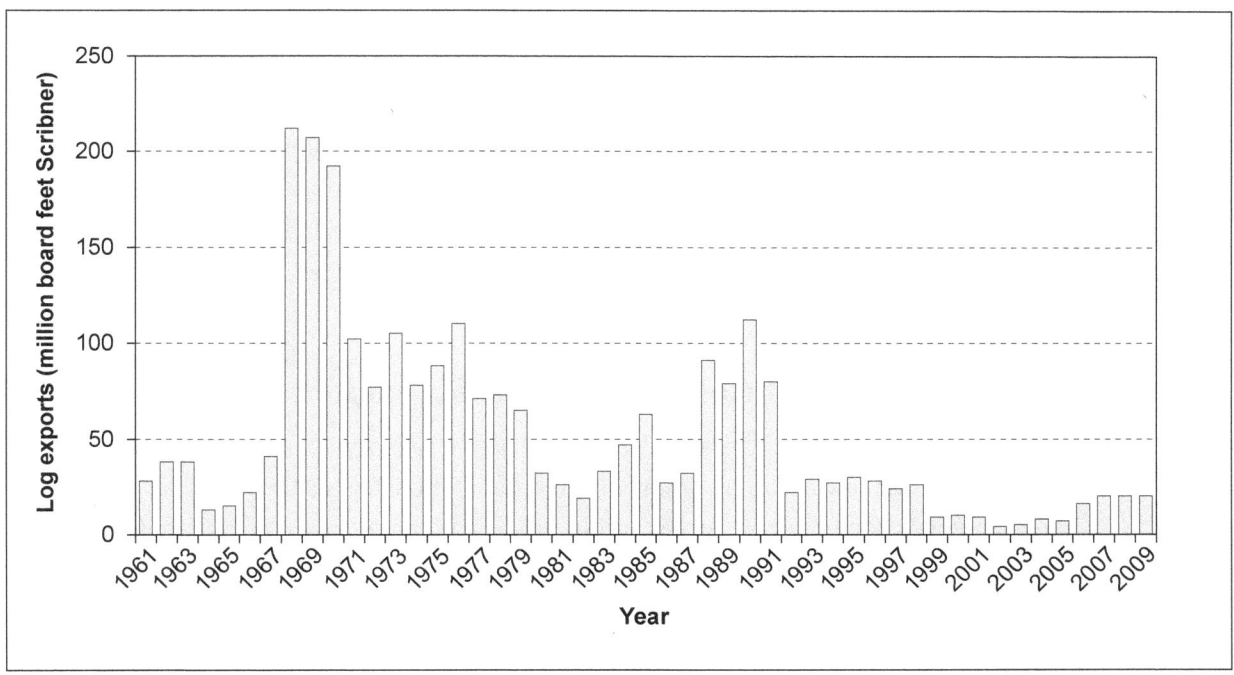

Figure 8—California's international log exports, 1961–2009 (WWPA 1964–2009).

Table 12—California timber flow by resource area, 2006

Harvest area	Receiving area					
	North Coast and Central Coast[a]	Northern Interior[b]	Sacramento[c]	San Joaquin[d]	Out of state	Total harvest
	- - - - - - - - - - - - - - - - - *Million board feet Scribner* - - - - - - - - - - - - - - - - -					
North Coast and Central Coast[a]	439.4	65.7	8.5	0.1	1.4	515.1
Northern Interior[b]	21.0	453.1	73.4	—	59.7	607.2
Sacramento[c]	0.4	33.0	420.5	13.8	5.5	473.2
San Joaquin[d]	—	—	19.2	108.9	—	128.1
Southern California[e]	—	—	—	9.6	—	9.6
Out of state[f]	105.8	20.7	—	0	N/A	126.5
Total received	566.6	572.5	521.6	132.4	66.6	

N/A = not applicable.

[a] North Coast and Central Coast regions are combined to avoid disclosure. North Coast includes Del Norte, Humboldt, Mendocino, and Sonoma Counties and Central Coast includes Alameda, Contra Costa, Marin, Monterey, Napa, San Benito, San Francisco, San Mateo, Santa Clara, Santa Cruz, and Solano Counties.

[b] Northern Interior region includes Lassen, Modoc, Siskiyou, Shasta, and Trinity Counties.

[c] Sacramento region includes Butte, Colusa, El Dorado, Glenn, Lake, Nevada, Placer, Plumas, Sacramento, Sierra, Sutter, Tehama, Yolo, and Yuba Counties.

[d] San Joaquin region includes Alpine, Amador, Calaveras, Fresno, Kern, Kings, Madera, Mariposa, Merced, Mono, San Joaquin, Stanislaus, Tulare, and Tuolumne Counties.

[e] Southern California region includes Imperial, Inyo, Los Angeles, Orange, San Luis Obispo, Riverside, San Bernardino, San Diego, Santa Barbara, and Ventura Counties.

[f] Out-of-state region includes Oregon and Washington.

California mills was processed in the county where it was harvested, and 92 percent was processed in the resource area of harvest.

Timber harvest volume not processed within its county or resource area of origin tended to be delivered to the north or west, or to Oregon. This trend continued in 2006 with the Northern Interior resource area shipping the largest volume of timber to be processed out-of-area, mostly to Oregon and the Sacramento resource area. The Northern Interior resource area was a net exporting region, and the other resource areas were net timber importers.

Structure of California's Forest Products Industry

The 2006 FIDACS census identified 77 active primary wood and paper products facilities in California, producing an array of products that included lumber and other sawn products, veneer, utility poles, log home accents, medium-density fiberboard, particleboard, hardboard, bioenergy, and decorative bark (fig. 9, table 13). The number of primary processors dropped from 93 in 2000 with the bulk of the losses in the lumber producing (i.e., sawmill) sector. Since the 2000 mill census, the number of veneer facilities remained at two, pulp and board facilities decreased with the closure of one pulpmill and two board plants, and producers of "other products" increased with the addition of a log home accent manufacturer.

The higher number of timber-processing facilities in 2000 versus the 1994 survey (Ward 1997) was due primarily to the inclusion of the bioenergy and decorative bark sectors in the 2000 and 2006 censuses, offsetting declines in the number of sawmills and pulp and board facilities. The bioenergy and decorative bark sectors included 25 and 10 facilities, respectively, in both 2000 and 2006.

The number of primary plants operating in California over the 38 years prior to 2006 decreased dramatically (table 13). Most of the change has been in the sawmill sector, but large changes have also occurred in the plywood and veneer sector as

Table 13—Active California primary wood products facilities by sector, 1968–2006

Industry sector	1968	1972	1976	1982	1985	1988	1992	1994	2000	2006
Sawmills	216	176	142	101	89	93	56	53	47	33
Veneer and plywood	26	25	21	10	6	6	3	4	2	2
Pulp and board	17	18	7	10	11	11	9	12	7	4
Bioenergy	b	b	b	b	b	b	b	b	25	25
Decorative bark	b	b	b	b	b	b	b	b	10	10
Other[a]	3	13	13	9	9	9	5	6	2	3
Total	262	232	183	130	115	119	73	75	93	77

[a] Other includes log home accent producers and shake and shingle manufacturers, as well as post, pole, and piling manufacturers.
[b] Data unavailable for bioenergy and decorative bark sectors for 1968 to 1994.
Source: Barrette et al. 1970; Hiserote and Howard 1978; Howard 1974, 1984; Howard and Ward 1988, 1991; Morgan et al. 2004; Ward 1995, 1997.

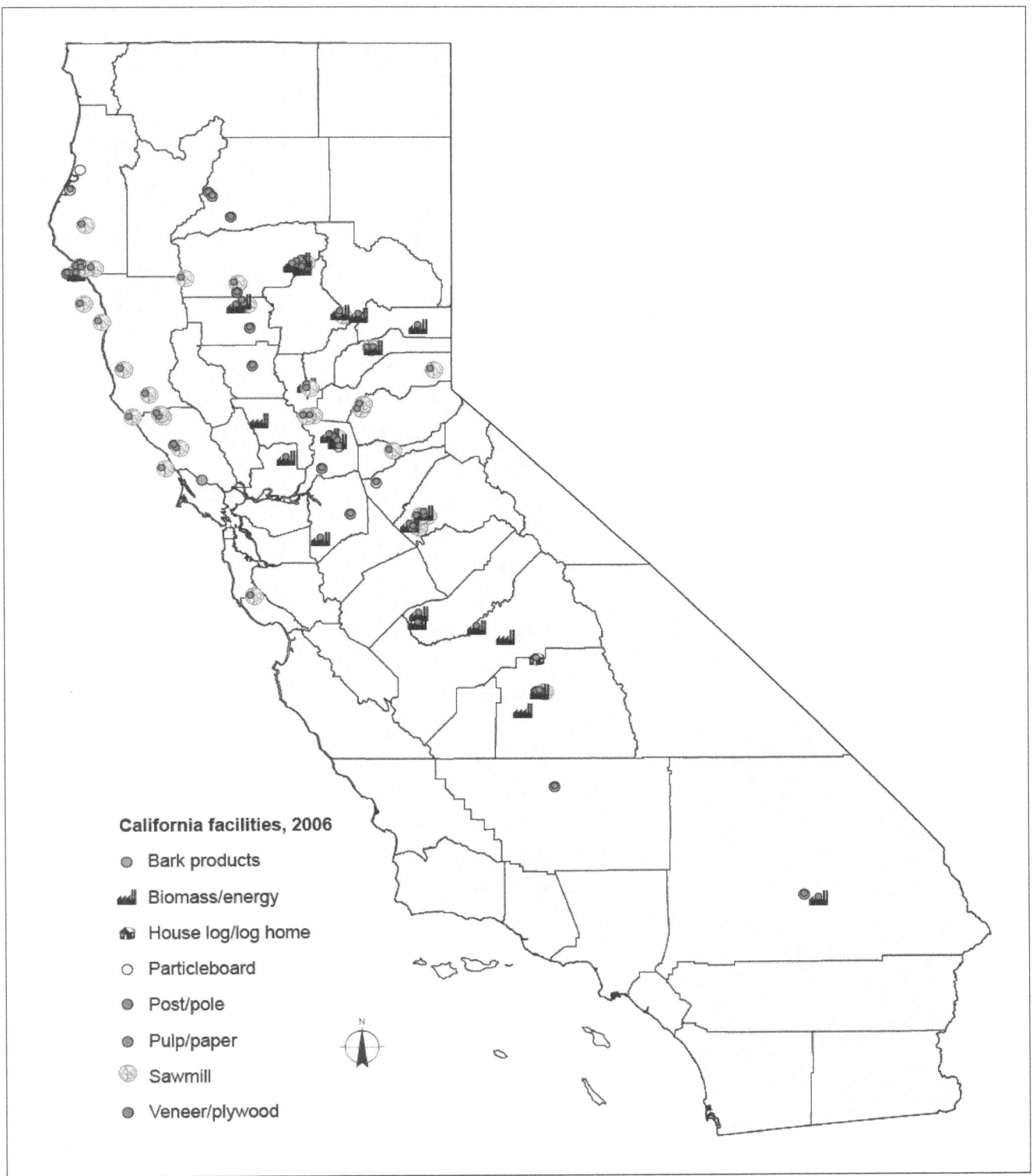

California facilities, 2006

- ⦿ Bark products
- 🏭 Biomass/energy
- 🏠 House log/log home
- ○ Particleboard
- ⦿ Post/pole
- ⦿ Pulp/paper
- ⦾ Sawmill
- ⦿ Veneer/plywood

Figure 9—Timber-processing facilities active in California during 2008.

well as in the pulp and board sector. The last 50 years have witnessed extensive closures of smaller and less competitive mills, especially those unable to handle smaller logs, leading to the concentration of production capacity into larger, more efficient mills. Between 1988 and 2006, the continued reduction in the number of sawmills was due primarily to reduced timber availability, with a considerable number of larger mills closing. Similar market forces affected California's plywood and veneer and pulp and board sectors; both now contain only a fraction of the mills that operated 40 years ago. With very poor market conditions since 2006, about eight additional major primary wood products facilities have closed at least temporarily (Ehinger 2009, Spelter et al. 2007). More detail on individual sectors is provided in the subsequent discussion.

Wood and paper product manufacturing facilities operated in 29 of California's 58 counties in calendar year 2006 (table 14). There were 10 active primary timber-processing facilities in Humboldt County in 2006, down from 15 facilities in 2000. Shasta County also had 10 active plants during 2006 compared to 14 in 2000. Tuolumne and Tulare Counties each contained more than four active primary timber-processing plants in 2006. Tuolumne had six processors, the same as in 2000, and Tulare had five facilities in 2006 versus two in 2000. In 2000, Mendocino and Sonoma Counties had eight and six facilities, respectively, and by 2006 each had only four.

As mentioned earlier, the distance that California's timber harvest travels to be processed is increasing. This increase is a result of reductions in both the volume harvested and the number of facilities that process timber. Similar reductions in harvested volumes and local milling infrastructure have occurred in the Interior West states (Arizona, Colorado, Idaho, Montana, New Mexico, Utah, and Wyoming). Previously unanticipated but potentially important consequences of increasing haul distances from forest to primary processors include an increase in fossil fuel consumption and corresponding decrease in net carbon sequestration by the forest products industry (Healey et al. 2009). The loss of milling infrastructure thus potentially reduces the ability to manage forests and carbon stocks but also reduces the potential efficiency of carbon sequestration by the forest products industry.

The total sales value reported by California's primary forest products plants in 2006 was about $1.5 billion, down from $2.6 billion in 2000 (table 15). Product prices in 2006 were about even with 2000; the loss is due to closure of mills and resultant lower production capacity. The FIDACS system provides sales value information for the entire primary forest products industry in 2000 and 2006. Published annual sales data for California's primary forest products industry are consistently

Table 14—Active California primary wood products facilities by county and sector, 2006

County	Sawmills	Veneer	Medium-density fiberboard and particleboard	Bioenergy	Decorative bark	Other[a]	Total
Amador	—	—	1	—	—	—	1
Butte	1	—	—	1	—	—	2
Del Norte	—	—	1	—	—	—	1
El Dorado	1	—	—	—	—	—	1
Fresno	—	—	—	2	—	—	2
Glenn	—	—	—	—	1	—	1
Humboldt	7	—	1	1	—	1	10
Kern	—	—	—	—	1	—	1
Lassen	—	—	—	3	—	—	3
Madera	—	—	—	1	—	—	1
Mendocino	4	—	—	—	—	—	4
Nevada	1	—	—	—	—	—	1
Placer	1	—	1	2	—	—	4
Plumas	2	—	—	2	—	—	4
Riverside	—	—	—	1	1	—	2
Sacramento	—	—	—	—	1	—	1
San Joaquin	—	—	—	1	1	—	2
Santa Cruz	1	—	—	—	—	—	1
Shasta	4	—	—	5	—	1	10
Sierra	—	—	—	1	—	—	1
Siskiyou	—	2	—	—	1	—	3
Sonoma	3	—	—	—	1	—	4
Sutter	1	—	—	—	—	—	1
Tehama	—	—	—	—	1	—	1
Trinity	1	—	—	—	—	—	1
Tulare	1	—	—	2	1	1	5
Tuolomne	3	—	—	2	1	—	6
Yolo	—	—	—	1	—	—	1
Yuba	2	—	—	—	—	—	2
2006 total	33	2	4	25	10	3	77
2000 total[b]	47	2	5	25	10	4	93

[a] Other includes log home accent producers and shake and shingle manufacturers, as well as post, pole, and piling manufacturers.
[b] Source: Morgan et al. 2004.

Table 15—Sales value of California's primary wood products, 2000 and 2006

Product	2000[a]	2006
	Thousands of 2006 U.S. dollars	
Lumber, timber, and associated products	1,711,173	984,723
Residue-utilizing sector[b]	532,082	257,321
Bioenergy	298,426	201,404
Veneer and other primary wood products[c]	88,350	96,294
Total	2,630,031	1,539,742

[a] Source: Morgan et al. 2004.
[b] Residue-utilizing sector includes pulp, paper, and board manufacturers, and decorative bark.
[c] Veneer and other products include log home accents, peeler cores, posts, poles, pilings, and veneer.

Sawmill sector continues to be the largest component of California's primary forest products industry in terms of sales value and volume of timber processed.

available only for lumber. To put these values in perspective, we estimated lumber sales values for previous years using reported lumber sales (WWPA 1964–2009), historical production data, trends in the Annual Survey of Manufactures (USDC CB 2009), and descriptions of industry sectors in previous industry studies (Morgan et al. 2004). The annual sales value of California's primary forest products (free on board the producing mill) would have exceeded $4 billion (in constant 2006 dollars) for several years in the 1960s and 1970s.

Sawmill Sector

California's sawmill sector continues to be the largest component of California's primary forest products industry in terms of sales value (table 15) and volume of timber processed (table 8). The 33 sawmills operating in California during 2006 accounted for slightly less than 7 percent of domestic softwood lumber production, which equates to about 4 percent of U.S. lumber consumption (WWPA 1999–2009).

Lumber production in California peaked at 6 billion board feet (fig. 10) during the late 1950s, concurrent with the post-World War II housing boom. Production dropped to about 5 billion board feet and held near that level throughout the 1960s and 1970s. With advancing technology, sawmills were able to recover more lumber

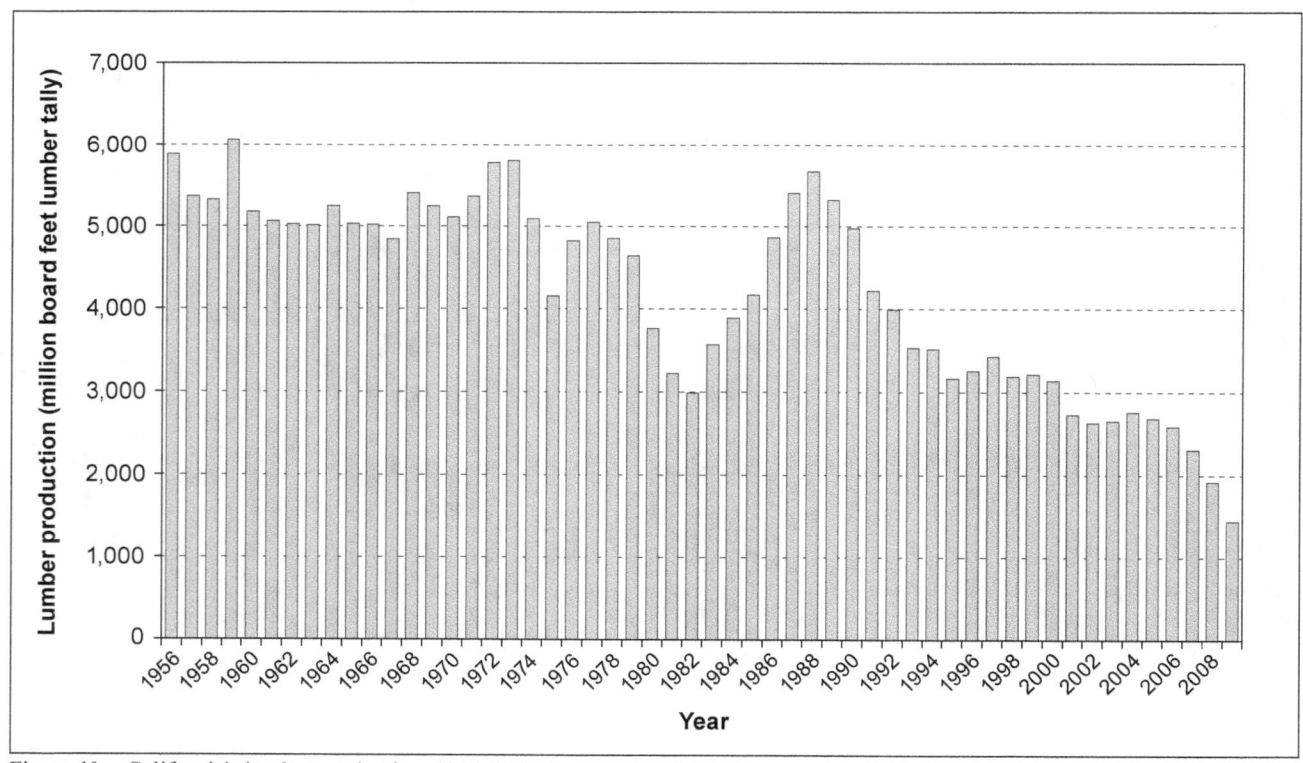

Figure 10—California's lumber production, 1956–2009 (WWPA 1964–2009).

from the logs processed and offset the slightly lower overall timber harvest and increased use of timber by the plywood industry (Keegan et al. 2010a). Very strong markets maintained average annual lumber production above 5 billion board feet throughout the 1970s, and annual sales value exceeded $4 billion during four years of the decade (fig. 11).

In late 1979, there was an abrupt and extreme downward shift in wood products markets brought on by a severe recession of the post-World War II period. The early 1980s were a time of very low prices, and in the recession of 1982, California lumber production fell to 2,987 MMBF, with sales of $1.6 billion. In 1988, California sawmills rebounded with lumber production of 5,671 MMBF and sales of $3.0 billion, owing to a strong national economy, a temporary abundance of sold-but-not-yet-cut federal timber, and continued increases in lumber recovery per unit of timber processed.

During the 1990s, sawmills struggled with declining timber availability. Timber harvest levels on national forests in California fell by more than 60 percent, and 50 of the state's 93 sawmills closed between 1988 and 1994. Lumber production in 1994 was 3,521 MMBF, down 38 percent or nearly 2.2 MMBF from 1988. With good markets and high lumber prices, sales value fell by only 26 percent (figs. 9 and 10). After strong markets in 1999, the economy weakened in 2000 and timber

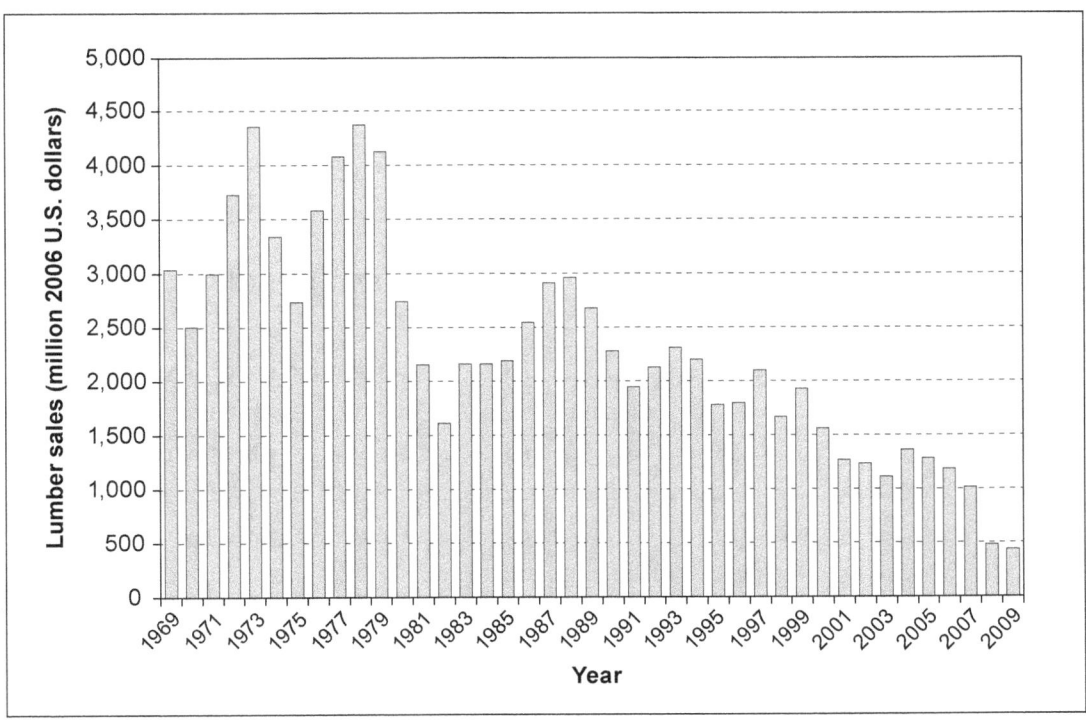

Figure 11—California's inflation-adjusted lumber sales, 1969–2009 (WWPA 1964–2009).

availability continued to deteriorate on public and private lands. Lumber production for 2000 dropped to 3.1 billion board feet with a sales value of $1.6 billion. The declines continued into the decade; despite very strong housing and lumber markets in 2004 and 2005, output and sales value were below 2000 levels. With weakening markets in 2006, output fell to 2.6 billion board feet, and lumber sales value was at $1.2 billion. The housing and lumber market weakness continued into 2009. California's lumber production volume and sales value were estimated to be 1.9 billion board feet and $482 million for 2008 (WWPA 2009), with another 25-to 30-percent drop anticipated by the end of 2009.

Veneer and Plywood Sector

Currently there are no plywood plants in California and only two plants producing veneer for further manufacture into plywood and laminated-veneer lumber (LVL) by mills located in Oregon. The plywood sector was relatively short-lived in California. It emerged and almost completely disappeared in the course of 60 years. With strong wood markets and the development of technology to make quality plywood out of abundant large-diameter Douglas-fir timber, California plywood production grew rapidly in the 1950s and early 1960s, peaking in 1964 at 1.3 billion square feet (3/8-inch basis). A number of factors have accounted for the decline and near disappearance of California's plywood and veneer industry. Howard (1974) points out that large-diameter Douglas-fir logs became less available. At the same time, spikes in log exports in the late 1960s and early 1970s brought increased competition for logs (Morgan et al. 2004). More recently, substitute products such as oriented strand board captured large portions of construction markets once dominated by plywood. Details about California's two remaining veneer plants cannot be discussed to avoid disclosure of firm-level information.

Residue-Utilizing Manufacturers—Pulp and Board, and Bark Facilities

During 2006, there were 15 facilities in California manufacturing products from the mill residue from sawmills and other plants that process timber into products. These included a pulp mill, four reconstituted board plants—three particleboard plants and a medium-density fiberboard facility—and 10 bark plants producing landscaping products such as decorative bark and mulch. Since 2000, the number of manufacturers using mill residues declined from 17 after the closure of a hardboard plant and a pulp and paper mill.

California's 2006 timber harvest included approximately 59 MMCF of bark, of which roughly 42 MMCF was used to produce energy and about 17 MMCF was used for other products such as mulch and landscaping bark. As with other mill residue in California during 2006, only a very small amount (less than 0.05 MMCF) of bark was not used.

Bark facilities are a relatively new addition to California's forest products industry. Prior to the early 1970s, the bark removed from timber during the production of lumber and other primary products was usually burned onsite for fuel, buried in landfills, or burned as waste. A market developed by the nursery and gardening industry led to the establishment of three decorative bark producers by 1975; this number grew to 10 by 2000 and remained at 10 in 2006.

Sales of residue-utilizing manufacturers totaled nearly $257 million in 2006, down from nearly $532 million in 2000. Most of the decline in sales resulted from the closures of the pulp mill and board plant, with sales from these producers dropping from $462 million in 2000 to $217 million in 2006. Sales from bark producers totaled about $40 million in 2006, down from $53 million in 2000. The decline in bark sales is likely because of the decline in timber harvest and processing statewide, making bark unavailable in some parts of the state.

Bioenergy Sector

The bioenergy sector in California in 2006 contained a variety of facilities, including cogeneration plants at timber-processing facilities such as sawmills that produced steam and electricity, as well as stand-alone facilities producing electricity using various mixes of urban and agricultural waste, sawmill residue, and timber. In 2006, 25 bioenergy facilities used some type of wood fiber, including roundwood, forest chips (i.e., trees or slash chipped in the forest), and sawmill residues. Just two facilities operated exclusively on sawmill residues; six used a mixture of agricultural waste, urban waste, and sawmill residue; and 17 facilities used forest chips, sawmill residue, and urban and agricultural waste.

The energy-producing capacity of the 25 bioenergy facilities that used wood fiber in 2006 totaled 485 megawatts (MW). Seven facilities are rated at 10 MW or less, six are between 10 and 20 MW, and 12 are greater than 20 MW. These producers sold close to 3.1 million megawatt hours (MWh) of power in 2006. One megawatt hour equals about one month's power consumption for about 1,000 typical California homes (California Energy Commission 2003). Nearly all of the energy produced was sold within the state of California. This was also the case in 2000. The total sales value was about $201 million (table 15) or about $0.0645 per kilowatt hour (KWh) on average.

As the pulp and board sectors have declined, the bioenergy sector has become more important to the forest products industry in California as a source of additional revenue for residue-producing facilities and for utilization of slash and other low-value forest material. Measured in cubic feet, the bioenergy sector used about 24 percent of the wood fiber (including bark) from California's timber harvest. This includes over 60 MMCF of timber harvested for energy and 33 MMCF or 350,000 BDU (nearly 25 percent) of California's mill residues, including bark.

Other Sectors

The remaining primary wood products manufacturers identified in 2006 included one house log accent facility and a utility pole producer. The number and type of facilities comprising California's "other" (wood product) manufacturers have varied throughout the years (table 13). Historical information on their operations is limited. These producers were typically small operations that come and go with demand for their products, making it challenging to determine the total number of facilities operating and obtain information from them. Because of the limited number of facilities, no production data for these firms can be reported, and sales data are included with the veneer sector.

Plant Capacity

This section focuses on capacity to process timber—specifically sawtimber—from 1988 through 2007 and the utilized proportion of that capacity. California's sawtimber-processing plants include sawmills, veneer mills, houselog facilities, and utility pole plants. Capacity for 2006 was developed from the FIDACS census of California's forest products industry. Capacity for previous years was estimated from previous industry censuses (Howard and Ward 1991, Morgan et al. 2004, Ward 1995) and for intervening years based on reported mill closures openings and expansions (Ehinger 2009, Random Lengths 2007, Spelter et al. 2007).

Sawtimber Processing Capacity

Through the FIDACS census, California mills were asked for their 8-hour shift and annual production capacities, given sufficient supplies of raw materials and firm market demand for their products. Large sawmills and veneer mills expressed annual production capacity equal to two to three 8-hour shifts daily for 240 to 300 operating days per year. Smaller mills generally reported annual capacity at only one shift per day, for not more than 250 days per year.

Sawmill production capacity was reported in thousand board feet lumber tally. Veneer production capacity was reported in thousands of square feet on a 3/8-inch basis, utility pole capacity was reported in lineal feet of poles, and houselogs used for log home accents were reported in number of pieces. To combine capacity figures for the state's sawtimber users and to estimate the industry's total capacity to process sawtimber, capacity was expressed in units of raw material input

(MMBF of timber Scribner Decimal C) and was called processing capacity. Sawmill capacity figures were adjusted to million board feet of timber Scribner Decimal
C log scale by dividing production capacity in lumber tally by the mill's calculated
lumber recovery per board foot Scribner. For veneer plants, production capacity in
square feet of 3/8-inch veneer was divided by each mill's calculated veneer recovery
figure. Capacities for utility pole plants were adjusted to thousand board feet Scribner by multiplying capacity in lineal feet by an average Scribner board-foot volume
per lineal foot. For log home accents, an estimate was made using the average
volume of a log that would be used for that product. These pieces were comparable
in size to veneer and sawlogs.

California's capacity to process timber in 2006 was an estimated 2.05 billion
board feet Scribner, of which 78 percent was used by mills processing just over 1.6
billion board feet (fig. 12). Several mill closures in 2007 reduced capacity. Although
this decline was somewhat offset by expansion at a number of existing facilities, it
appears that, in 2007, capacity to process sawtimber fell to about 1.9 billion board
feet. During 2008 and 2009, additional sawmill closures occurred and annual
timber-processing capacity dropped below 1.8 billion board feet.

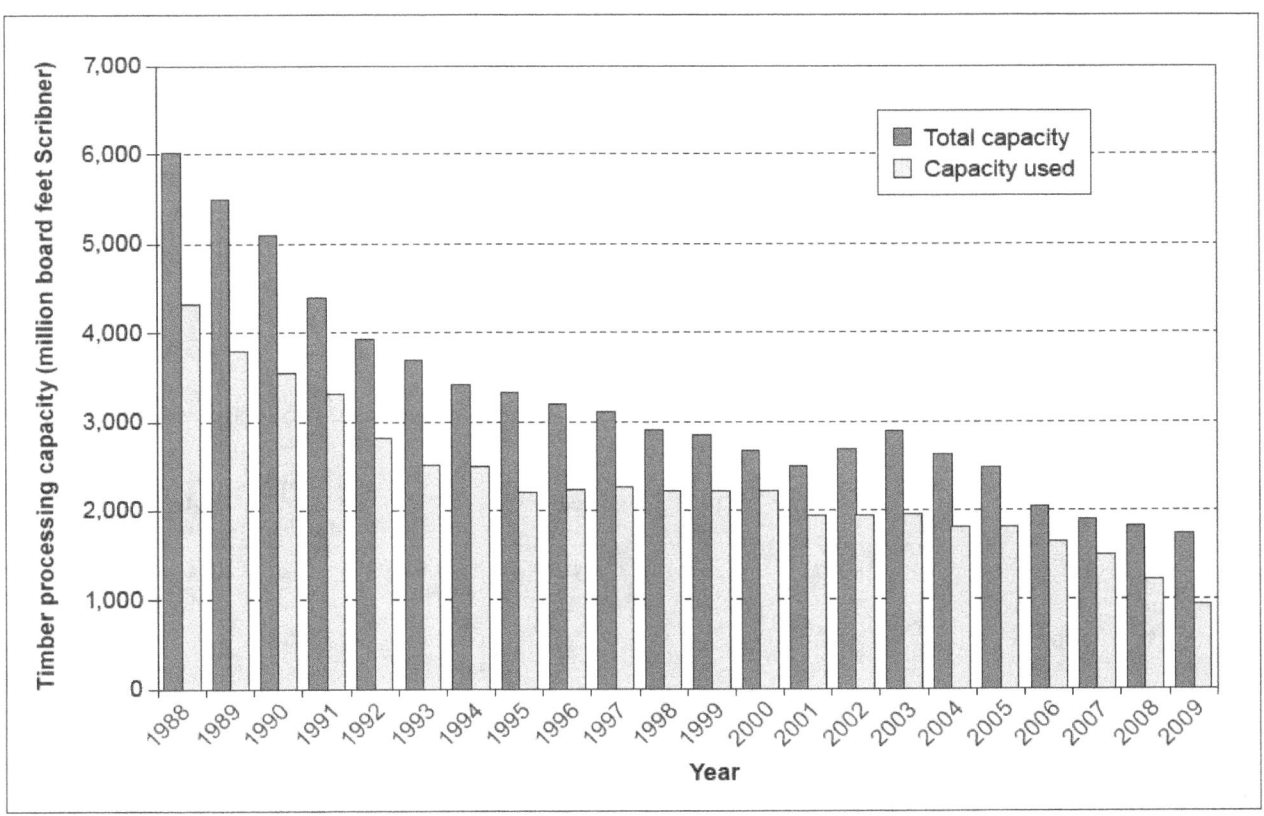

Figure 12—California's capacity for processing sawtimber, 1988–2009.

There has been a 70-percent drop in capacity to process sawtimber in California since 1988, when capacity was 6 billion board feet of log input, and mills processed approximately 4 billion board feet of timber. The major decline in capacity took place from 1988 to 1999 with a fall from 6 billion board feet to 2.8 billion board feet (Morgan et al. 2004). The capacity decline in the 1990s resulted primarily from the decline of 2 billion board feet in federal timber offerings. Also negatively affecting capacity during the 1990s and beyond were a series of increased state regulations of timber harvest activities, which effectively reduced the available private timber volume and increased costs. Changes in use of private lands—such as development, urbanization, or purchases/set asides for parks or old-growth preservation—have also contributed to reduced timber harvest from private forest lands. During the recent poor markets, the portion of capacity used has fallen more dramatically than has total capacity, from around 80 percent in the 2000 to 2006 period to an estimated 55 percent in 2009.

Lumber-Production Capacity

Capacity to produce lumber varies widely among California's 33 sawmills, and the proportion of capacity utilized is highly correlated with mill size (table 16). Total lumber production during 2006 was 2,453 MMBF and production capacity was 3,067 MMBF lumber tally. Thus, approximately 80 percent of California's annual lumber-producing capacity was utilized, which is nearly identical to 2000, when 81 percent was utilized. The majority, 2,178 MMBF (71 percent) of lumber-producing capacity, was concentrated in the 13 largest mills, with over 100 MMBF annual capacity. The degree of concentration of capacity among these mills increased from 2000, when 58 percent of capacity was in this size class. During 2006, these largest mills accounted for 75 percent (1,846 MMBF) of lumber production in California,

Table 16—Number of active California sawmills, capacity, production, and proportion of capacity used, by capacity size class, 2006

Capacity size class	Number of mills	Capacity	Percentage of total capacity	Average capacity per mill	Production	Percentage of total production	Average production per mill	Capacity used
		$MMBF^a$	Percent	$MMBF^a$	$MMBF^a$	Percent	$MMBF^a$	Percent
10 MMBF or less	5	10.5	0.3	2.1	6.6	0.3	1.3	63.0
Over 10 to 50 MMBF	5	113.2	3.7	22.6	70.6	2.9	14.1	62.4
Over 50 to 100 MMBF	10	765.6	25.0	76.6	530.3	21.6	53.0	69.3
Over 100 MMBF	13	2,178.0	71.0	167.5	1845.8	75.2	142.0	84.7
2006 total	33	3,067.2	100.0	92.9	2453.3	100.0	74.3	80.0
2000 total[b]	47	3,878.5	100.0	82.5	3137.7	100.0	66.8	80.9

[a] Volume in million board feet (MMBF) lumber tally.

[b] Source: Morgan et al. 2004.

and utilized 85 percent of their lumber-producing capacity on average. Mills with capacities of 50 to 100 MMBF accounted for 765 MMBF (25 percent) of total capacity, produced 530 MMBF (22 percent) of the state's lumber, and on average utilized about 70 percent of their capacity. This size class lost the most mills between 2000 and 2006, going from 18 mills to 10. The remaining 10 sawmills accounted for approximately 4 percent (124 MMBF) of California's lumber-producing capacity and about 3 percent (71 MMBF) of the state's lumber production. These smallest mills utilized the smallest proportion (about 62 percent) of their available capacity.

Lumber Recovery Factors and Overrun

Product recovery ratios, or the volume of output per unit of input, are reported for California's sawmills as lumber recovery factors (LRFs) and overrun. The LRF is the lumber output (in board feet lumber tally) divided by the timber input (in cubic feet). Overrun is the volume of lumber (in board feet lumber tally) actually obtained from a log in excess of the estimated volume based on log scale (board feet Scribner). Both are measures of mill efficiency. The volume of sawtimber used by California's sawmills in 2006 was approximately 300 MMCF, and lumber production was 2,473 MMBF lumber tally. Thus the statewide LRF for California sawmills in 2006 was 8.2 board feet of lumber output per cubic foot of log input, which is up from approximately 7.96 in 2000 (Morgan et al. 2004) and 7.2 in the 1970s (Keegan et al. 2010b).

Increases in LRF are attributable primarily to improvements in technology. Technological improvements have made California mills more efficient in numerous ways. For example, log size (diameter and length) sensing capabilities linked to computers determine the best sawing pattern for logs to recover either the greatest volume or greatest value from each log. Improved sawing accuracies have reduced the amount of size variation in sawn lumber, reducing the need for planing and increasing solid wood recovery. Thinner kerf saws reduce the proportion of the log that becomes sawdust, and curved sawing technology has increased recovery from logs with sweep and crook.

During 2006, California sawmills produced 2,473 MMBF lumber tally by processing 1,510 MMBF, Scribner Decimal C, of logs yielding an overrun of 64 percent or 1.64 board feet of lumber per board foot Scribner of log input. A comparison of California sawmill overrun for various years is shown in table 17.

Although overrun is the more common measure, it is not as useful as LRF because of the weakness of the Scribner scale as a measure of log input. The average size of logs processed in California has almost certainly decreased over the

Table 17—Overrun for selected years

	1968	1972	1976	1982	1985	2000	2006
Lumber overun	1.14	1.23	1.32	1.27	1.39	1.53	1.64

Source: Barrette et al. 1970; Hiserote and Howard 1978; Howard 1974, 1984; Howard and Ward 1988; Morgan et al. 2004.

past 50 years. As log diameters decrease, the Scribner log rule underestimates by an increasing amount the volume of lumber that can be recovered from a log, often increasing overrun.

Mill Residue: Quantity, Type, and Use

As indicated earlier in this report, about 60 percent of the wood fiber (including bark) processed by primary forest products plants ends up as mill residue. This residue can either present difficult and expensive disposal problems or be used to create additional products or energy to generate revenue. California's substantial bioenergy industry is the largest consumer of wood residues generated in the state, whereas sawmills are the largest residue producers.

Three types of wood residues are typically created by California's primary wood products industry: coarse or chippable residue consisting of slabs, edging, trim, log ends, and pieces of veneer; fine residue consisting primarily of planer shavings and sawdust; and bark. The 2006 census gathered information on volumes and uses of mill residue. Actual residue volumes, reported in bone-dry units (BDU), were obtained from facilities that sold all or most of their residues. One BDU is the equivalent of 2,400 pounds of oven-dry wood. All mills reported, on a percentage basis, how their residue was used.

Residue volume factors, which express mill residue generated per unit of output produced, were derived from production and residue output volumes reported by mills. California's sawmills produce the majority of residues during their normal production process. Residue factors for 2000 and 2006 are shown in table 18 and represent statewide averages. During 2006, sawmills in California produced less residue per thousand board feet (MBF) of lumber produced with both lower amounts of coarse residue and planer shavings generated. Several factors can

Table 18—California's sawmill residue factors, 2000 and 2006

Type of residue	2000[a]	2006
	Bone-dry units per MBF[b]	
Coarse	0.41	0.37
Sawdust	0.15	0.15
Planer shavings	0.13	0.11
Bark	0.23	0.21
Total	0.92	0.85

[a] Source: Morgan et al. 2004.
[b] Bone-dry units (2,400 pounds of oven-dry wood) of the various residue types generated for every thousand board feet of lumber manufactured.
MBF = thousand board feet.

contribute to changes in mill residue production. In general, changes in the size and species mix of logs received and products produced by sawmills can cause residue factors to change (Keegan et al. 2010a, 2010b). Improved milling technology tends to reduce the amount of planer shavings, sawdust, and coarse residue generated per unit of lumber, while decreases in average log size can increase the volume of coarse residue generated. Also, demand for mill residue from the residue-utilizing sector can affect sawmill residue production, with sawmills allowing more residue (particularly coarse residue like clean chips) to be produced when demand for residue is relatively high and demand for lumber products is relatively low.

In 2006, California sawmills generated more than 2.1 million BDU of mill residue, accounting for nearly 91 percent of all mill residues generated that year (tables 19 and 20). The remaining 9 percent of mill residue production came from veneer plants, utility pole facilities, and log home accent plants.

Coarse residue was the state's largest component of wood products residue (table 20). Facilities in California produced 1,005,542 BDU of coarse residue; only 12 BDU were not used for some purpose. About 54 percent of coarse residue was used by the pulp and reconstituted board plants, 40 percent was used to produce energy, and about 6 percent was sold and used for other products.

Fine residues—sawdust and planer shavings—made up 25 percent of residue (656,818 BDU) in 2006. Sawdust composed 60 percent and planer shavings 40 percent of fine residue. All fine residue was used in some fashion, primarily as fuel (399,746 BDU) or in reconstituted board products (157,786 BDU). California facilities generated 610,503 BDU of bark while processing timber in 2006—all but 0.05 percent of which was used by other sectors. Seventy-three percent of bark (442,328 BDU) was used for bioenergy, and 27 percent (167,933 BDU) was used as landscaping or soil additives.

Table 19—Volume of wood residue generated by California's sawmills, 2006

	Wood residue			Percentage of type		Percentage
Residue type	Used	Unused	Total	Used	Unused	of total
	- - - - - - - *Bone-dry units.*- - - - - - -			- - - - - - - - - -*Percent*- - - - - - - - - - -		
Coarse	918,231	—	918,231	100	—	100
Fine						
Sawdust	363,560	—	363,560	100	—	100
Planer shavings	264,258	—	264,258	100	—	100
Bark	531,349	227	531,576	99.96	0.04	100
Total	2,077,398	227	2,077,625	99.9	0.01	100

Table 20—California's production and disposition of wood products residue, 2006

Type of residue[a]	Total utilized	Pulp and board	Energy	Landscape products, animal bedding, and other uses	Unutilized	Total produced
	- *Bone-dry units* -					
Coarse	1,005,530	540,573	401,227	63,730	12	1,005,542
Fine						
Sawdust	392,560	68,267	281,666	42,626	—	392,560
Planer shavings	264,258	89,519	118,080	56,660	—	264,258
Bark	610,261	—	442,328	167,933	242	610,503
All residue	2,272,609	698,359	1,243,301	330,949	253	2,272,862
	- *Percentage of residue by residue type* -					
Course	99.99	53.8	39.9	6.3	<.01	100
Fine						
Sawdust	100.00	17.4	71.8	10.9	—	100
Planer shavings	100.00	33.9	44.7	21.4	—	100
Bark	99.96	—	72.5	27.5	0.04	100
All residue	99.99	31.1	54.7	14.6	0.01	100

[a] Includes residue from the manufacture of lumber, veneer, utility poles, and houselogs.

Forest Product Sales, Employment, and Worker Earnings

California's primary wood products sales, including bioenergy, totaled slightly more than $1.5 billion in 2006.

At nearly $1.1 billion and 70 percent of total sales, California is its own largest market for wood and paper products.

Mills responding to the FIDACS survey summarized their calendar year 2006 shipments, providing information on volume, sales value, and geographic destination of finished wood products. Mills usually distributed their products either through their own distribution channels or through independent wholesalers and selling agents. Because of subsequent transactions, the geographic destination reported here may not reflect final delivery points of shipments. The map in figure 13 shows the regions where California's manufactured wood products were distributed in 2006. Canada and the Pacific Rim destinations are not shown on the map.

The 2006 census collected market information by geographic destination and product type (table 21). California's primary wood products sales, including bioenergy, totaled slightly more than $1.5 billion in 2006. Sales of lumber and sawn products accounted for 64 percent of total sales, slightly less than $985 million. The residue-utilizing sector accounted for 17 percent ($257 million) of sales, bioenergy sales made up 13 percent ($201 million), and other products made up the other 6 percent ($96 million).

At nearly $1.1 billion and 70 percent of total sales, California is its own largest market for wood and paper products. The majority (75 percent) of lumber remains in the state, whereas just over half (52 percent) of output from the residue-utilizing sector is retained in-state. Almost all of the energy and electricity produced by the

Figure 13—Shipment destinations of California's primary wood products. Regions are California (1), Far West (2), Rocky Mountains (3), North Central (4), South (5), and Northeast (6).

Table 21—Destination and value of California's primary wood products sales, 2006

Product	California	Far West	Rocky Mountains	North Central	Northeast	South	Other[a]	Total
				- - - - - *Thousands of 2006 U.S. dollars* - - - - -				
Lumber, timbers, and associated products	737,984	52,017	73,611	65,691	29,935	21,457	4,029	984,723
Residue-utilizing sector[b]	133,510	8,728	9,008	2,183	91	835	102,965	257,321
Energy and electric	201,328	77	—	—	—	—	—	201,404
Veneer and other primary wood products[c]	385	91,257	851	—	—	—	3,800	96,294
2006—All primary wood products	1,073,207	152,079	83,470	67,874	30,026	22,292	110,795	1,539,742
2000—All primary wood products[d]	1,418,295	263,675	177,091	213,285	83,975	59,693	77,445	2,293,459

[a] Other destinations include the Pacific Rim and Canada.

[b] Residue-utilizing sector includes facilities that use residues from the manufacture of lumber and other products, including pulp mills, board facilities, and bark plants.

[c] Veneer and other primary wood products include log home accents, peeler cores, pencil stock, utility poles, and veneer.

[d] Source: Morgan et al. 2004.

bioenergy sector are also used in-state. Veneer and other primary wood products are sold in higher proportions out of state with 95 percent of veneer and other products sold to the Far West states. The sale of veneer to plywood and LVL mills in Oregon accounts for much of these sales.

The Far West states make up the second largest market for primary wood products made in California, at $152 million or 10 percent of 2006 sales; primarily through lumber and veneer sales. About 5 percent of all lumber is bought by users in these states, and lumber constitutes 34 percent of sales to the region. The Rocky Mountain States accounted for 5 percent of California's primary forest industry sales, the majority of it (88 percent) in the form of lumber. The North Central states received 4 percent of total sales value, again most of it as lumber (97 percent). Sales to the Northeast totaled just over $30 million, or about 2 percent of total California primary wood product sales, while sales to the South approached $23 million, or a little over 1 percent.

Exports constituted a larger percentage of California's total primary wood products sales in 2006 relative to earlier years. An estimated $111 million in products went to Canada and the Pacific Rim countries, about 7 percent of total sales; this compares to $ 77 million or 4 percent in 2000. The bulk ($103 million) of sales to foreign countries during 2006 was generated from the residue-utilizing sector.

Employment and Worker Earnings in California's Forest Products Industry

Employment data reported in the FIDACS mill census were used in conjunction with employment and earnings data from the U.S. Department of Commerce Regional Economic Information System to identify employment and labor income for California's primary and secondary forest products industry. Labor income is generally a more reliable measure of economic activity than employment because of the often substantial differences in earnings per worker. The primary forest products industry includes logging, processing logs into lumber and other wood products, processing wood residues from timber-processing plants into outputs such as paper or electricity, and private sector forest management services. The secondary industry, as defined in this report, includes the further processing outputs (e.g., manufacturing windows or doors from lumber) from the primary industry, although the outputs may be from California or elsewhere. The FIDACS census was then used to more precisely identify the proportion of the total wood and paper products industry classified as primary and to provide additional detail by sector and geographic region within California.

Starting in 1997, most of the primary and secondary wood products industry is reported in the North American Industry Classification System (NAICS). The forest products industry can be found in four categories: NAICS 113—forestry and logging; NAICS 1153—forestry support activities; NAICS 321—wood product manufacturing; and NAICS 322—paper manufacturing. Prior to 2001, most of the industry could be found in three standard industrial classifications (SIC) as defined by the U.S. Office of Management and Budget: SIC 08—forestry services; SIC 24—lumber and wood products; and SIC 26—pulp, paper, and allied products. Industry totals are not completely comparable between the SIC and NAICS systems. To remedy this discrepancy, the U.S. Department of Commerce Bureau of Economic Analysis has made state-level personal income information available in NAICS from 1990 to 2006, thus allowing enough years for reasonable time series with the data (USDC BEA 2009). These classifications were used to estimate total direct employment and income to workers (labor income) in California's forest products industry. They provide a conservative representation of the wood and paper products industry, as they capture the majority of the primary and secondary activity. However, a number of activities (i.e., hauling of logs and other raw materials by independent truckers; hauling of finished products by truck, rail, or barge; and forest management activities related to timber production by government employees) involving several thousand workers are not included in these NAICS sectors.

Based on the four NAICS sectors (113, 1153, 321, and 322), approximately 78,100 workers (fig. 14), earning more than $4.4 billion annually (fig. 15), were directly employed in the primary and secondary wood and paper products industry, including logging, in California during 2006 (USDC BEA 2009). Consequently, average worker earnings across California' primary and secondary wood products industries were about $52,400 per year. These employment and earnings figures do not include indirect or induced economic impacts, which have suggested that every direct job supports an additional 1.5 jobs (Phillips 2006).

About 15,000 workers were employed in the harvesting and processing of timber or in private sector land management, and they earned about $680 million in labor income. The remaining component of the industry can be classified as secondary and employed about 63,000 workers in 2006, with worker earnings of approximately $3.4 billion. The secondary wood and paper industry relies on the output of the primary industry from California and other parts of the world for raw materials.

Total employment in California's wood and paper products industry has decreased since 1990, when employment was over 105,000. Trends in labor income show similar declines from about $4.8 billion (in 2006 dollars) in labor income

Approximately 78,100 workers earning more than $4.4 billion annually were directly employed in the wood and paper products industry, including logging, in California during 2006.

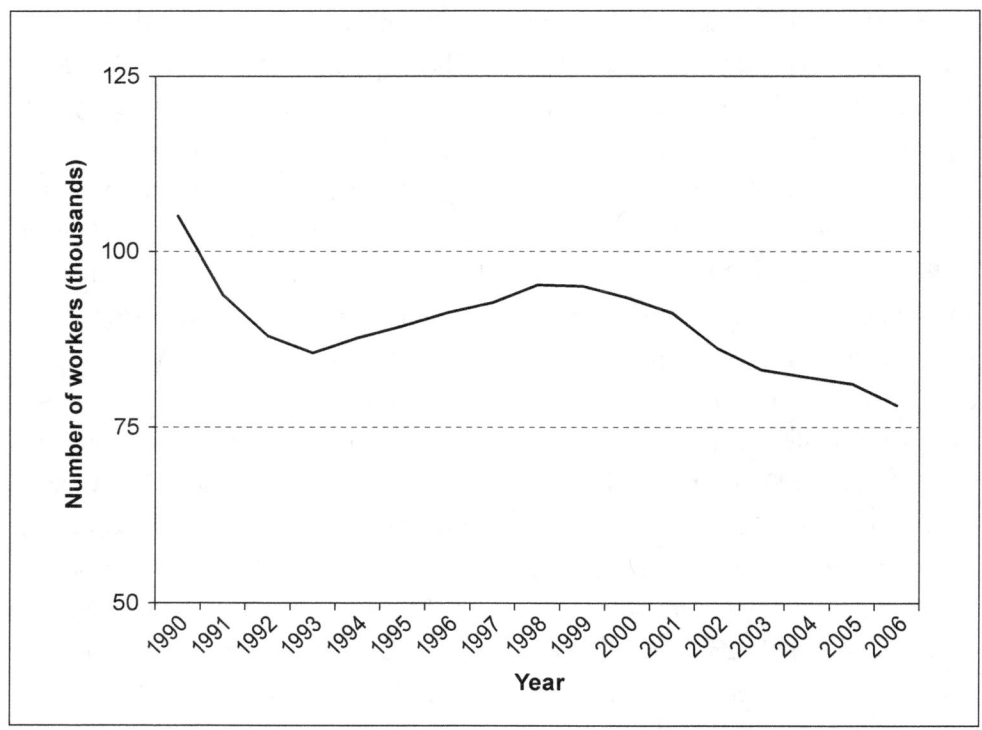

Figure 14—Employment in California's wood and paper products industry, 1990–2006.
Source: U.S. Department of Commerce Bureau of Economic Analysis (2009).

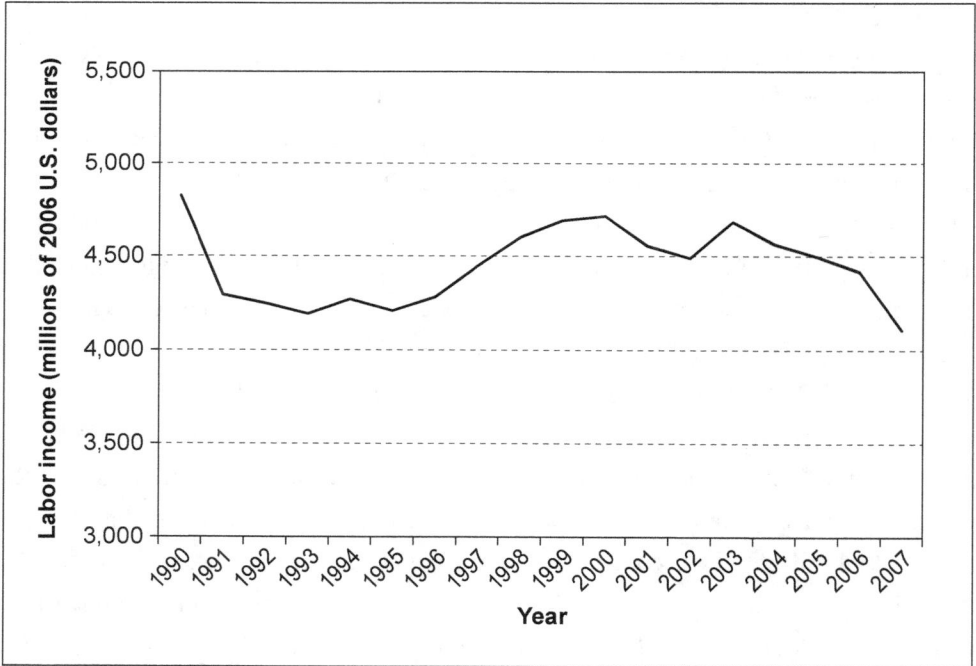

Figure 15—Adjusted labor income in California's wood and paper products industry, 1990–2007.
Source: U.S. Department of Commerce Census Bureau (2009).

in 1990 to $4.4 billion in 2006. These long-term decreases have resulted almost entirely from losses in the primary industry. From 1990 to 2006, overall employment in California's wood and paper products industry declined by nearly 27,000 workers. Over this period, primary industry employment fell from about 39,000 workers in 1990 to about 15,500 in 2006 (table 22). This 60-percent decline in employment in California over the last three decades is attributed mostly to declines in timber harvest and availability, and some impacts from increased mill efficiency as discussed earlier. This was compounded by the persistent economic downturn and housing decline in more recent years.

Although the total number of workers employed in California's primary and secondary industry has been declining since the 1990s, the number of workers employed per MMBF (Scribner) of timber harvested increased fairly dramatically during the 1990s (fig. 16). Sharp declines in the volume of timber harvested in California and timber exports from California (see figs. 2 and 7) along with dramatic increases in timber imports and growth in the secondary industry contributed to the increase in workers per MMBF of timber harvested. Since 2001, employment per MMBF of timber harvested has been gradually declining. This decline may be a result of continued low levels of timber harvest resulting in more attrition in the primary sector in concert with a generally steeper rate of employment decline across the entire industry. The 2008/2009 economic recession is expected to further reduce employment as demand for housing and virtually all wood and paper goods has declined. This will likely reduce employment per MMBF of timber harvested, although a return to early 1990s levels is unlikely.

Forest Industry Employment and Labor Income in California

California's secondary wood and paper products industry is concentrated near population centers in the state's southern and central counties. The primary forest products industry is concentrated in the northern counties, closer to where timber harvesting occurs. About 75 percent of the primary industry is concentrated among

Table 22—California's primary wood products industry employment, selected years

Sector	1990	2000	2006
Logging and forest management	19,000	10,000	8,000
Sawmills and veneer facilities	12,000	6,000	5,000
All other manufacturers	8,000	4,000	2,500
Total primary employment	39,000	20,000	15,500

Source: U.S. Department of Commerce, Bureau of Economic Analysis (2009).

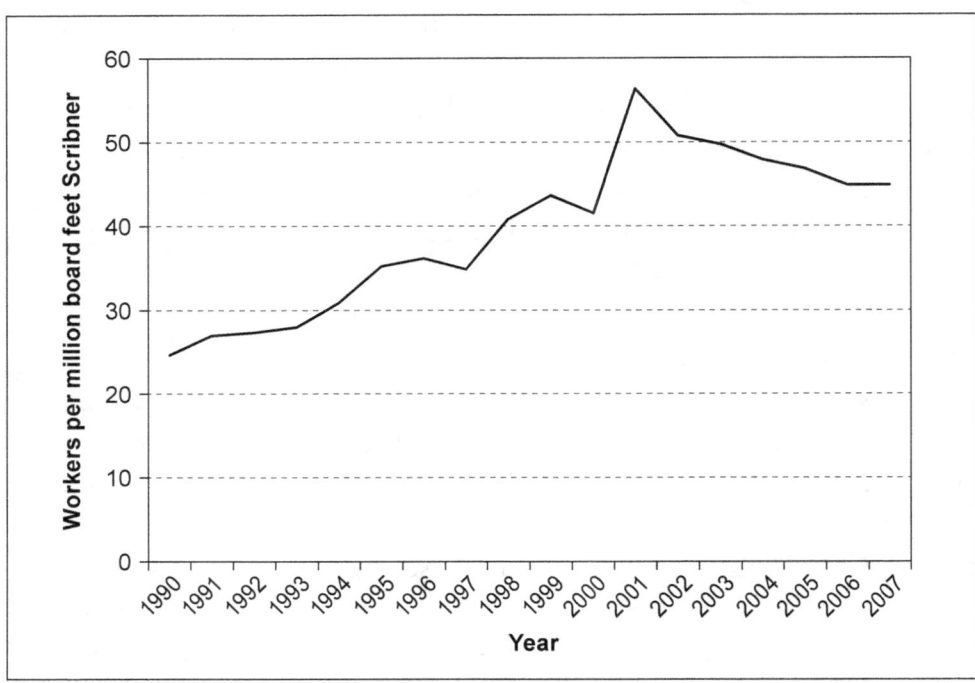

Figure 16—Employment per unit volume of timber harvested in California, 1990–2007.
Source: U.S. Department of Commerce Bureau of Economic Analysis (2009).

11 contiguous northern counties (i.e., Del Norte, Humboldt, Lassen, Mendocino, Modoc, Plumas, Shasta, Sierra, Siskiyou, Tehama, and Trinity). These 11 northern counties are home to only 1.7 percent of the state's population, about 1.2 percent of labor income, and 1.5 percent of the state's employment. However, these counties contain more than 65 percent of primary forest products industry workers, earning over $535 million (70 percent) of labor income.

During 2006, approximately 4 percent of total employment and 5 percent of the 11-county region's total labor income of $535 million was in the primary and secondary wood and paper products industry. Considering associated industries and indirect impacts, industry likely accounts for 10 percent of earnings by people engaged in the work force in these counties. Based on percentage of total labor income during 2006, Sierra County had the highest concentration of wood and paper products in its economy at 11 percent. Humboldt County, with the largest industry concentration, had 7 percent of total labor income directly in wood and paper products.

During the 1970s, the wood and paper products industry accounted for over 20 percent of direct total labor income and over 33 percent of the economic activity in these counties. However, with the declines in the wood and paper products industry described earlier and diversification of the region's economy, direct labor income fell to just over 12 percent in 1990. By 2000, 8.8 percent of the region's total labor income was directly in the wood and paper products industry, and by 2006 that dropped to 5 percent. So while these 11 northern counties remain a very important part of California's wood products industry, declines in the industry, particularly in the primary sector, can disproportionately affect the region. Consequently, policymakers and others with concerns for the wood products industry should be aware that statewide policies and legislation, whether related to the environment, labor, or industry, will generally have larger impacts on the residents of these northern counties than on the state's population as a whole.

Metric Equivalents

When you know:	Multiply by:	To find:
Inches	2.54	Centimeters
Feet	0.3048	Meters
Miles	1.609	Kilometers
Acres	0.405	Hectares
Square feet	0.0929	Square meters
Square feet per acre	0.229	Square meters per hectare
Cubic feet	0.0283	Cubic meters
Cubic feet per acre	0.06997	Cubic meters per hectare
Ounce	28349.5	Milligrams
Pounds	0.453	Kilograms
Pounds per cubic foot	16.018	Kilograms per cubic meter
Tons per acre	2.24	Megagrams per hectare
Degrees Fahrenheit	$(°F - 32)/1.8$	Degrees Celsius
British thermal units (Btu)	.000293	Kilowatt hours
Pounds per cubic foot	.016	Grams per cubic centimeter

References

Barrette, B.R.; Gedney, D.R.; Oswald, D.D. 1970. California timber industries, 1968: mill characteristics and wood supply. Sacramento, CA: California Department of Conservation, Division of Forestry. 117 p.

California Energy Commission. 2003. Glossary of energy terms. http://www. energyquest.ca.gov/glossary/index.html. (March 7, 2003).

California State Board of Equalization. 1978–2007. California timber harvests. Timber Yield Tax Program. http://www.boe.ca.gov/proptaxes/timbertax.htm. (December 1, 2008).

Christensen, G.A.; Campbell, S.J.; Fried, J.S., tech. eds. 2008. California's forest resources, 2001–2005: five-year Forest Inventory and Analysis report. Gen. Tech. Rep. PNW-GTR-763. Portland, OR: U.S. Department of Agriculture, Forest Service, Pacific Northwest Research Station. 183 p.

Ehinger, P.F. 2009. Personal communication. Consulting forester, Paul F. Ehinger & Associates, 2300 Oakmont Way, #212, Eugene, OR 97401.

Hartman, D.A.; Atkinson, W.A.; Bryant, B.S.; Woodfin, R.O. 1981. Conversion factors for the Pacific Northwest forest industry. Seattle, WA: University of Washington, College of Forest Resources, Institute of Forest Products. 112 p.

Healey, S.P.; Blackard, J.A.; Morgan, T.A.; Loeffler, D.; Jones, G.; Brandt, J.P.; Moisen, G.G.; DeBlander, L.T. 2009. Changes in timber haul emissions in the context of shifting forest management and infrastructure. Carbon Balance and Management. 4(9). doi:10.1186/1750-0680-4-9.

Hiserote, B.A.; Howard, J.O. 1978. California's forest industry, 1976. Resour. Bull. PNW-RB-80. Portland, OR: U.S. Department of Agriculture, Forest Service, Pacific Northwest Forest and Range Experiment Station. 95 p.

Howard, J.O. 1974. California forest industry: wood consumption and characteristics, 1972. Resour. Bull. PNW-RB-52. Portland, OR: U.S. Department of Agriculture, Forest Service, Pacific Northwest Forest and Range Experiment Station. 91 p.

Howard, J.O. 1984. California forest industry: 1982. Resour. Bull. PNW-RB-119. Portland, OR: U.S. Department of Agriculture, Forest Service, Pacific Northwest Forest and Range Experiment Station. 79 p.

Howard, J.O.; Ward, F.R. 1988. California's forest products industry: 1985. Resour. Bull. PNW-RB-150. Portland, OR: U.S. Department of Agriculture, Forest Service, Pacific Northwest Research Station. 72 p.

Howard, J.O.; Ward, F.R. 1991. California's forest products industry: 1988. Resour. Bull. PNW-RB-181. Portland, OR: U.S. Department of Agriculture, Forest Service, Pacific Northwest Research Station. 69 p.

Keegan, C.E.; Morgan, T.A.; Blatner, K.A.; Daniels, J.M. 2010a. Trends in lumber processing in the western United States, part 1: board foot Scribner volume per cubic foot of timber. Forest Products Journal. 60 (2): 133–139.

Keegan, C.E.; Morgan, T.A.; Blatner, K.A.; Daniels, J.M. 2010b. Trends in lumber processing in the western United States, part 2: overrun and lumber recovery factors. Forest Products Journal. 60 (2): 140–143.

Miles, P.D.; Hansen, M.H. 2008. Forest inventory EVALIDator web-application version 1.0. St. Paul, MN: U.S. Department of Agriculture, Forest Service, Northern Research Station. http://199.128.173.26/evalidator/tmattribute.jsp. (February 2009).

Morgan, T.A.; Keegan, C.E.; Dillon, T.; Chase, A.L.; Fried, J.S.; Weber, M.H. 2004. California's forest products industry: a descriptive analysis. Gen. Tech. Rep. PNW-GTR-615. Portland, OR: U.S. Department of Agriculture, Forest Service, Pacific Northwest Research Station. 55 p.

Phillips, R.H. 2006. Jobs and income associated with resource and recreation outputs. In: Charnley, S., tech. coord., Northwest Forest Plan: The first ten years (1994–2003): socioeconomic monitoring results. Volume III: Rural communities and economies. Gen.Tech. Rep. PNW-GTR-649. Portland, OR: U.S. Department of Agriculture, Forest Service, Pacific Northwest Research Station: 37–51.

Random Lengths. 1976–2009. Forest product market prices and statistics yearbook. Eugene, OR: Random Lengths Publications, Inc.

Random Lengths. 1993. Terms of the trade. Eugene, OR: Random Lengths Publications, Inc. 351 p.

Random Lengths. 2006. Big book 2006: the buyers and sellers directory of the forest products industry. Eugene, OR: Random Lengths Publications, Inc. 1168 p.

RISI. 2006. 2007 Lockwood-Post directory of the pulp, paper, and allied trades. San Francisco, CA: 793 p.

Society of American Foresters. 1998. The Dictionary of forestry. Helms, J.A., ed. Bethesda, MD. 210 p.

Spelter, H.; McKeever, D.; Alderman, M. 2007. Profile 2007: Softwood sawmills in the United States and Canada. Res. Pap. FPL-RP-644. Madison, WI: U.S. Department of Agriculture, Forest Service, Forest Products Laboratory. 65 p.

Steer, H.B. 1948. Lumber production in the United States, 1799–1946. Misc. Publ. 669. Washington, DC: U.S. Department of Agriculture, Forest Service. 233 p.

U.S. Department of Commerce, Census Bureau (USDC CB). 2009. Annual Survey of Manufactures (ASM). http://www.census.gov/mcd/asmhome.html/. (June 2009).

U.S. Department of Commerce, Bureau of Economic Analysis (USDC BEA). 2009. Regional Economic Information System (REIS). http//www.bea.gov/regional/reis/. (February 2009).

Ward, F.R. 1995. California's forest products industry: 1992. Resour. Bull. PNW-RB-206. Portland, OR: U.S. Department of Agriculture, Forest Service, Pacific Northwest Research Station. 68 p.

Ward, F.R. 1997. California's forest products industry: 1994. Resour. Bull. PNW-RB-217. Portland, OR: U.S. Department of Agriculture, Forest Service, Pacific Northwest Research Station. 60 p.

Western Wood Products Association [WWPA]. 1964–2009. Statistical yearbook of the Western lumber industry. Portland, OR. Annual.